SpringerBriefs in Computer Science

For further volumes:
http://www.springer.com/series/10028

James H. Laros III · Kevin Pedretti
Suzanne M. Kelly · Wei Shu
Kurt Ferreira · John Van Dyke
Courtenay Vaughan

Energy-Efficient High Performance Computing

Measurement and Tuning

 Springer

James H. Laros III
Sandia National Laboratories
Albuquerque, NM
USA

Kevin Pedretti
Sandia National Laboratories
Albuquerque, NM
USA

Suzanne M. Kelly
Sandia National Laboratories
Albuquerque, NM
USA

Wei Shu
Electrical and Computer Engineering
  Department
University of New Mexico
Albuquerque, NM
USA

Kurt Ferreira
Sandia National Laboratories
Albuquerque, NM
USA

John Van Dyke
Sandia National Laboratories
Albuquerque, NM
USA

Courtenay Vaughan
Sandia National Laboratories
Albuquerque, NM
USA

ISSN 2191-5768   ISSN 2191-5776 (electronic)
ISBN 978-1-4471-4491-5   ISBN 978-1-4471-4492-2 (eBook)
DOI 10.1007/978-1-4471-4492-2
Springer London Heidelberg New York Dordrecht

Library of Congress Control Number: 2012944978

Printed on acid-free paper

Springer is part of Springer Science+Business Media (www.springer.com)

For my father—James H. Laros Jr.

Foreword

I am very pleased to contribute a foreword for this monograph authored by James H. Laros III, Kevin Pedretti, Suzanne M. Kelly, Kurt Ferreira, John Van Dyke, and Courtenay Vaughan from Sandia National Laboratories, and Professor Wei Shu from the University of New Mexico. James led this high-performing team and is a staff member in my department who has worked many years on research for the integration and development of "first of a kind" High Performance Computing (HPC) systems. One of these systems was Red Storm, a National Nuclear Security Administration (NNSA), Office of Advanced Simulation and Computing (ASC), capability computing system. Red Storm was the prototype and progenitor of Cray Corporation's line of XT3/4/5 massively parallel processor supercomputers. Sandia is proud of the collaboration we established with Cray to design and develop Red Storm technology and contribute to Cray's commercial success. As described in this book, the Red Storm system management infrastructure provided a unique ability to collect high-resolution energy measurements. These application-centric energy usage profiles provide insight into the issues and trade-offs that must be addressed using advanced concepts for future energy-efficient HPC systems. This monograph is very timely because energy consumption is an increasingly important issue for all HPC systems and the applications they support.

The objective function for HPC is changing from a singular focus on *time to solution* to include a balanced consideration of both *time and energy to solution*. This is a significant change. Historically, high performance computing has always been concerned with performance, with a principal metric of time to solution. Energy challenges appeared in 2004 with the appearance of the first dual-core processor. However, it is only in the last several years, that the community has come to realize that HPC energy consumption is a very severe constraint. Energy is now a primary constraint that may limit the scale of a system we can afford to power.

This new objective function is expected to be a driver for optimization efforts that apply co-design principles from embedded computing to the design and development of future generations of HPC systems. These efforts will apply multidisciplinary collaboration on hardware/software co-design. The capabilities developed by this team's research can be useful for integration into a test bed to support the design and development of energy-efficient applications and algorithms. These capabilities can also be directly integrated into future production HPC systems that use an adaptive runtime system to dynamically monitor and control various hardware capabilities as HPC applications enter different phases of computation. The development of these advanced HPC concepts are a strategic area of research and development for Sandia.

I hope you will find this book a useful reference to aid in the design and development of future HPC systems. This monograph should also be useful for developers of energy efficient applications and algorithms, system software developers that are developing adaptive runtime software, computer architects that want to understand how applications will use future HPC systems, and HPC facility managers that are trying to understand the power requirements for future systems.

James A. Ang Ph.D.
Manager, Scalable Computer
Architectures Department
Sandia National Laboratories
Albuquerque, NM, USA

Preface

In the summer of 2007 we discovered, very much by accident, that the hardware on Red Storm might contain the instrumentation necessary to monitor both the current draw and voltage of board level components. Red Storm, the first instance of the Cray XT architecture line, was the result of a collaboration between Sandia National Laboratories and Cray Inc. Due to this collaboration, a few Sandia engineers had wide access to test both hardware and source code. The light-weight kernel operating system (Catamount) used in the experiments detailed in this book was in fact created by some of the authors of this book. Our virtually un-fettered access to the necessary hardware and software enabled the experiments you will find detailed herein.

Our research was directed toward increasing energy efficiency of large-scale High Performance Computing (HPC) platforms. While HPC, historically, has been a performance-driven sector of computing, it has been recognized that the *performance above all* trend cannot continue. A great deal of research has been conducted in related areas at a number of universities. While important and insightful, prior work did not focus on real scientific applications run at large-scale on production HPC platforms. Using the tools, hardware and software, made available by our collaboration we focused on conducting empirical studies that had high potential impact on energy efficiency. Our experiments included: evaluating power savings opportunities during idle periods, determining the impact of operating system noise on power usage and analyzing the trade-off between energy and performance while tuning the CPU frequency and network bandwidth. All experiments were conducted at large-scale using the fine-grained high-frequency in situ measurement capability developed specifically for this purpose.

While the material contained in this book is focused on large-scale HPC, a broader audience interested in power and energy efficiency in general might find utility in the information presented. What the reader will find amounts to a journal of major phases of our work in this area, each building on the success and lessons learned from previous experiments. Readers unfamiliar with this field of study in general will benefit from the introductory chapters and background presented in

Chaps. 1 through 4, while the more acquainted may want to go directly to the coverage of our experiments in Chaps. 5 through 7.

I have had the pleasure of working with most of the authors of this book for quite some time on a number of challenging projects and I remain humbled to be associated with each of them. Their contributions were essential to this research in a range of ways too extensive to list.

James H. Laros III
Principal Member of Technical Staff
Scalable Computer Architectures
Sandia National Laboratories
Albuquerque, NM, USA

Acknowledgments

The following agencies have provided funding directly or indirectly to this work: National Nuclear Security Agency (NNSA), Advanced Simulation and Computing (ASC) program, and the Department of Energy's (DOE) Innovative and Novel Computational Impact on Theory and Experiment (INCITE) program. Sandia National Laboratories Center 1420 Sudip Dosanjh, Senior Manager, Department 1422 James Ang, Manager and Department 1423 Ronald Brightwell, Manager.

The authors also recognize the contributions of the Sandia High Performance Computing (HPC) support staff: Dick Dimock, Barry Oliphant, Jason Repik, and Victor Kuhns; the production management: John Noe and Robert Ballance and the Oak Ridge support provided by Don Maxwell. A special thanks to Mark Swan of Cray Inc. for providing the basis of the software instrumentation used in our research.

Contents

Chapter 1
Introduction

Abstract There are many motivations driving the desire for increased energy efficiency. While many sectors share similar motivations, the High Performance Computing (HPC) sector must address a different set of challenges in achieving energy efficiency. This chapter will outline some of the motivations of this research along with the approach taken to address these recognized challenges, specifically for large-scale platforms.

1.1 Motivation

There are three primary challenges in CPU chip architecture design [1]: memory [2], instruction level parallelism [3], and power. Of these, power is the primary technology barrier which influenced chip manufactures towards multi-core designs. Recently a study was commissioned by the Defense Advanced Research Projects Agency (DARPA) to investigate the technology challenges that must be overcome to achieve an ExaFLOP in computation. In this study four major challenges were identified. Power was recognized as *"the most pervasive of the four"* [4].

The power used by a CMOS circuit is, at this point in time, dominated by dynamic power. As feature sizes shrink, static power (power due to leakage current) will increasingly become an important factor. In addition, the vast majority of power introduced into the chip must be removed in the form of heat. As feature sizes shrink, this becomes more difficult. More heat must be removed from a smaller area. Addressing these issues (and others) for mobile and server CPU chip architectures has long-established motivations.

For large platforms, the impact of reducing power on reliability could have important implications. In related works Feng [5] and Ge [6] conclude that power has a direct relationship to reliability as stated by Arrhenius' Law [7]. Pinheiro in an extensive study done at Google [8] states evidence to the contrary showing no strong correlation between temperature and the reliability of spinning disk. Intuitively,

J. H. Laros III et al., *Energy-Efficient High Performance Computing*,
SpringerBriefs in Computer Science, DOI: 10.1007/978-1-4471-4492-2_1,
© James H. Laros III 2013

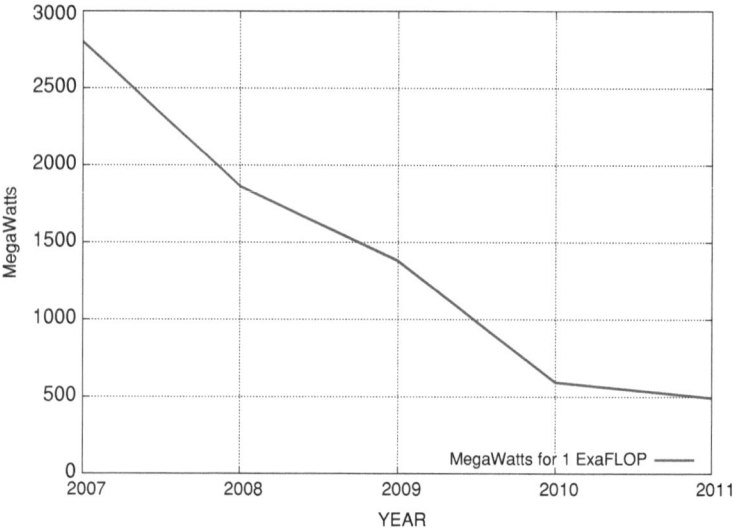

Fig. 1.1 Megawatts of power needed for a 1 ExaFLOP based on Green 500 most efficient platform

it would seem that components with moving parts would be more likely affected by temperature than a CPU, for example. Hsu in [9], however, claims informal empirical data supports Arrenhius' equation as applied to cluster systems. If reducing power can be conclusively proven to have a positive impact on platform reliability this alone would provide a huge motivation.

The High Performance Computing (HPC) community has for many years ignored power as a major factor in favor of increased performance. While expensive, on the order of a million dollars per megawatt year, the power budget has been considered as a cost of doing business. Expensive facilities have been constructed to house large HPC platforms in climate controlled environments to more efficiently remove the increasing amount of heat resulting from the increasing amount of power required by modern processors. If this trend continues, annual power costs will soon equal or surpass acquisition costs of next generation platforms. Figure 1.1 depicts the amount of power in megawatts that the most efficient platform, based on the Green 500 list, would require to achieve 1 ExaFLOP. As can be seen, great improvements have been made between 2007 and 2011 but as of 2011 an ExaFLOP platform would require nearly 500 megawatts of power. Powering this platform for one year would exceed the cost of most if not all HPC platforms.

Existing hardware has been successfully leveraged by present day operating systems to conserve energy whenever possible but these approaches have proven ineffective and even detrimental at large scale for most scientific computing applications. While hardware must provide a large part of the solution, the manner in which hardware is leveraged on large-scale platforms requires a new and flexible approach. It is particularly important that any approach taken has a system-level, rather than node-level, view of these issues.

1.2 Overview

In response to this challenge a thus far unique ability to measure current draw and voltage, in situ, on a large HPC platform at a very fine granularity and high frequency has been developed. The first experiment begins with the goal of reducing power consumption during idle cycles. This concept is extended to multi-core architectures by ensuring cores not in use remain in low power states during application execution. It is common for HPC applications to use fewer than the number of available cores per node. For many scientific applications, the memory wall in the form of capacity, capability or both, force users to limit the number of cores per node to better balance their application memory requirements at scale. While conserving power during idle cycles can produce large energy and related cost savings,[1] this research has additionally endeavored to explore possible energy efficiencies during application runtime on active CPU cores.

HPC applications are typically bulk synchronous. Savanella and Milazzo [10] describe the three execution phases of bulk synchronous programs as; computation, communication, and synchronization. Petrini et al. [11] and Ferreira et al. describe how operating system noise can effectively slow overall computation of bulk synchronous programs. In short, the runtime of an application will be throttled by the slowest MPI rank involved in a bulk synchronous computation. Allowing frequency changes that are dictated locally, rather than from the system's perspective, can cause the equivalent of operating system noise (or jitter) adversely affecting application performance.

To avoid this potential performance impact, the second experiment modifies CPU frequency during application execution, but employs a system-level perspective. Initially, it was assumed to achieve significant savings without unacceptable impacts in performance, frequency scaling would have to be performed during natural wait states in application execution. For example, during communication wait phases. This experiment concludes static frequency can produce large energy savings with little to no associated performance penalty.

The third and final experiment conducted takes advantage of the ability to tune the performance of the network components of a large-scale HPC platform. This research, combined with the results of previous experiments and analysis, demonstrates that a *sweet spot* exists for most, if not all, HPC applications run at large scale where maximum energy efficiency can be achieved without unacceptable performance trade-offs. A large amount of empirical data is provided to support this claim.

---

[1] These changes were applied to the production Red Storm capability class platform at Sandia National Laboratories and the Cray XT4 platform at Pittsburgh Supercomputer Center and have reduced power-related facility charges by an estimated one million dollars to date.

Evaluating acceptable trade-offs between energy efficiency and runtime performance is, of course, somewhat subjective. This research indicates that the parameters of these trade-offs are application, platform, and likely scale dependent. While the HPC community has traditionally prioritized performance above all metrics, future per-processor or per-platform power requirements will likely alter priorities and place more importance on energy efficiency metrics like FLOPS/watt or energy to solution. While this research is directed at exploring power and energy savings potential, performance remains a critical parameter of evaluation.

All experiments were conducted on two Cray XT class platforms; Red Storm located at Sandia National Laboratories and Jaguar hosted by Oak Ridge National Laboratory. The results of these experiments clearly indicate that opportunities exist to save energy by tuning platform components, individually or together, while maintaining application performance. The ultimate goal is to reduce energy consumption of real applications run at very large scale while minimizing the impact on runtime performance (defined for our purposes as wall-clock execution time).

References

1. S. Borkar, A.A. Chien, The future of microprocessors. Commun. ACM **54**(5), 67–77 (2011)
2. S.A. McKee, Reflections on the Memory Wall, in *Proceedings of the Conference on Computing Frontiers*, ser. CF '04. ACM, 2004
3. D.W. Wall, Limits of Instruction-Level Parallelism, in *SIGARCH Computer Architecture News*, ACM, vol. 19, 1991
4. K. Bergman, S. Borkar, D. Campbell, W. Carlson, W. Dally, M. Denneau, P. Franzon, W. Harrod, J. Hiller, S. Karp, S. Keckler, D. Klein, R. Lucas, M. Richards, A. Scarpelli, S. Scott, A. Snavely, T. Sterling, R. S. Williams, K. Yelick, *Exascale Computing Study: Technology challenges in achieving exascale systems peter kogge, editor& study lead*, 2008
5. X. Feng, R. Ge, K.W. Cameron, Power and Energy Profiling on Scientific Applications on Distributed Systems, in *IEEE Proceedings of the International Parallel and Distributed Processing Symposium (IPDPS)*, 2005
6. R. Ge, X. Feng, S. Song, H.-C. Chang, D. Li, K. Cameron, PowerPack: energy profiling and analysis of high-performance systems and applications. Trans. Parallel Distrib. Syst. **21**(5), 658–671 (2010)
7. M. White, Physics-of-Failure Based Modeling and Lifetime Evaluation, in *Microelectronics Reliability* (Jet Propulsion Laboratory, National Aeronautics and Space Administration, 2008)
8. E. Pinheiro, W-D. Weber, L.A. Barroso, Failure Trends in a Large Disk Drive Population, in *Proceedings of the 5th USENIX conference on File and Storage Technologies (USENIX)*, 2007
9. C. Hsu, W. Feng, Power-Aware Run-Time System for High-Performance Computing, in *Proceedings of the International Conference on High Performance Computing, Networking, Storage, and Analysis (SC)*, ACM/IEEE, 2005
10. A. Zavanella, A. Milazzo, Predictability of Bulk Synchronous Programs Using MPI, in *IEEE Proceedings of the Euromicro Workshop on Parallel and Distributed Processing*, 2000
11. F. Petrini, D. Kerbyson, S. Pakin, The Case of the Missing Supercomputer Performance: achieving optimal performance on the 8,192 processors of ASCI Q, in *Proceedings of the International Conference on High Performance Computing, Networking, Storage, and Analysis (SC)*, ACM/IEEE, 2003

Chapter 2
Platforms

Abstract The ability to quantify power and energy use is critical to understanding how power and energy are currently being used. A measurement capability is also necessary to measure the effect of tuning or modification of platform parameters, CPU frequency, and network bandwidth for example. In later chapters, these effects will be evaluated based on energy savings versus performance impact. Simply stated, power and energy measurement first require hardware support. This chapter will outline the hardware architectures and some of the significant systems software of the platforms used in the experiments detailed in this book.

2.1 Hardware Architecture

The experiments covered in this book were all accomplished on some variant of the Cray XT architecture. To our knowledge, this is the only platform that exposes the ability to measure current draw and voltage, in situ, as described in Chap. 3. Both the idle cycle and CPU frequency scaling experiments required specific operating system modifications to the Catamount [1] light-weight kernel (LWK). Catamount, authored by a team at Sandia National Laboratories, was the first production operating system available on the Cray XT line of supercomputers. Catamount support is currently limited to the Cray XT3 and XT4 variants of the architecture. The Cray XT architecture also affords the rare ability to tune performance parameters of other components. This capability is exploited to tune network bandwidth while measuring the effect on application energy in Chap. 6. The following sections will describe the specific test platforms and configurations in more detail. It is important to note that obtaining the dedicated time on production High Performance Computing (HPC) platforms to conduct experiments of this type is extremely difficult and very expensive.

J. H. Laros III et al., *Energy-Efficient High Performance Computing*,
SpringerBriefs in Computer Science, DOI: 10.1007/978-1-4471-4492-2_2,
© James H. Laros III 2013

2.1.1 Red Storm

Red Storm, the first of the Cray XT architecture line, was developed jointly by Cray Inc., and Sandia National Laboratories. The Cray XT architecture has been installed at numerous government and commercial sites including Oak Ridge National Laboratory. Red Storm is currently a heterogeneous architecture containing both dual and quad core processors. Both variants are used in the experiments discussed in this book. All nodes, dual and quad, are connected via a Seastar 2.1 network interface controller/router (Seastar NIC) in a modified mesh (mesh in X and Y directions and a torus in the Z direction).

Dual Core Nodes

The network bandwidth experiments described in Chap. 6 were accomplished on the dual core (XT3) partition of Red Storm. The XT3 partition contains 3,360 AMD 64 bit 2.4 GHz dual-core processors with 4 GB of DDR memory (2 GB per compute core). Each XT3 node is connected to the network via a Seastar NIC. The ability to manipulate the network bandwidth of the platform is equivalent on both the XT3 and XT4 partitions. The primary driver of using the XT3 partition for the network bandwidth experiments was simply the availability of this partition. The idle experiments were conducted on both the dual and quad core partitions of Red Storm.

Quad Core Nodes

Red Storm's XT4 partition utilizes AMD 64 bit 2.2 GHz quad-core processors with 8 GB of DDR2 memory (2 GB per compute core). Red Storm has 6,240 quad-core compute nodes, each connected to the network via a Seastar NIC. The frequency scaling experiments described in this book were conducted solely on the quad-core processors of either Jaguar or Red Storm due to the Advanced Power Management (APM) architectural requirements. The method of exploiting APM features will be discussed in Chap. 6. Some of the applications used in this research are export controlled and could not be executed on Jaguar (an open platform). Since the architectures and software stacks used were identical, we simply maximized our use of each platform based on application requirements and test platform availability.

2.1.2 Jaguar

Use of Jaguar was granted through the Department of Energy's Innovative and Novel Computational Impact on Theory and Experiment (INCITE) program. Jaguar, located at Oak Ridge Leadership Computing Facility (OLCF), was used for a portion of the frequency scaling experiments outlined in Chap. 6. The XT4 partition of Jaguar was specifically employed since it was both easier to gain dedicated access to and the architecture supported Catamount with much less up front effort than the XT5 partition would have required. Dedicated access was necessary for a number of reasons, primarily driven by our requirement to run Catamount (no longer a Cray supported operating system for the XT5 architecture and beyond). The XT4 partition of Jaguar contains 7,832 64 bit quad-core AMD Opteron processors (or nodes). Each core executes at 2.2 GHz and has access to 8 GB of DDR2 memory (2 GB per compute core). Each node on Jaguar is connected to the network via a Seastar NIC. The network topology of the Jaguar XT4 partition is a 3D torus. Jaguar's network topology, differs somewhat from Red Storm's modified mesh. These differences are not significant to the experiments conducted and had no affect on the results.

2.2 Operating System

Serial number one of the Cray XT architecture employed a light-weight kernel operating system named Catamount. For approximately four years, Catamount was delivered by Cray Inc. as the production operating system for the XT3 platform line. Catamount, at the time, was the latest in the lineage of light-weight operating systems authored, or co-authored, by Sandia National Laboratories.[1] Catamount was designed to get out of the way of the application. Important hardware abstractions and memory management are all provided with performance being the primary design consideration. When a parallel application is launched, Catamount provides the initial setup for the application, including contiguous memory allocation, and then suspends itself other than handling interrupt driven tasks such as those from network devices (Seastar NIC). This is a simplistic description but sufficient for the purposes of this book. Catamount is a small deterministic operating system in contrast with general purpose operating systems such as Linux. While it has proven to be a successful production operating system, Catamount has also proved invaluable for operating system and systems software research at Sandia National Laboratories.

The first experiment conducted was directed at saving energy during idle cycles since early versions of Catamount ignored this as a design consideration. The design of Catamount preceded many of the APM capabilities found on recent processor architectures. Once successful, later experiments explored further power efficiencies by leveraging more advanced APM features such as frequency scaling. The simplicity and deterministic nature of Catamount greatly aided in conducting these experiments. More detail on specific modifications will be included in our coverage as necessary.

---

[1] Sandia's most recent effort is the Kitten light-weight kernel [2].

2.3 Reliability Availability and Serviceability System

Historically, Reliability Availability and Serviceability (RAS) systems were commonly provided by vendors on mainframe class systems. Today, RAS systems look very different and are generally unique to high end custom HPC class architectures (Cray XT/XE and IBM BlueGene L/P and Q, for example). It is hard to define a clear line where cluster management systems become RAS systems. Generally, cluster management systems consist of a loose collection of open source utilities that are each individually designed for a narrow purpose. They are seldom well integrated and can often be intrusive to the primary purpose of the platform, computation. At small scale, the level of interference is often acceptable. RAS systems, in general, are typically more intentionally designed and integrated, often specific to a single architecture (in our opinion one of the failures of RAS system designs historically [3]).

The following are excerpts from the requirements for Cielo [4], a recent capability class procurement by the Alliance for Computing at Extreme Scale (ACES), a collaboration between Sandia National Laboratories and Los Alamos National Laboratory.

1. *To achieve delivery of the maximum continuous system resource availability, the RAS system must be a well engineered, implemented, and integrated part of the proposed platform.*
2. *There shall be a separate and fully independent and coherent RAS system.*
3. *The RAS system shall be a systematic union of software and hardware for the purpose of managing and monitoring all hardware and software components of the system to their individual potential.*
4. *Failure of the RAS system (software or hardware) shall not cause a system or job interrupt or necessitate system reboot.*

While this is only a small portion of the requirements that described and specified the RAS system for Cielo, it suggests some differentiating characteristics between a generic cluster management system and what is considered a RAS system. For these experiments, one of the most important characteristics is the separation but close integration of the RAS system in relationship to the underlying platform. This allows for the out-of-band scalable collection of current and voltage data necessary for all experiments included in this book. Out-of-band, in this context, means that control and monitoring of the platform, in general, is accomplished without affecting the platform or the software running on the platform. Measuring current and voltage data, for example, does not require an operating system interrupt using our methodology. It is very important that experimental methods do not, or minimally, affect the normal activity of the system. In a related work [5], laptops were employed to measure power using the operating system ACPI interface. This method causes an operating system interrupt each time a measurement is requested. While the interruption is minimal, at large scale this type of measurement could introduce the equivalent of operating system noise [6, 7]. There is no such interruption during the measurements used in in our experiments. The separate RAS network additionally allows the collection of these measurements in a scalable manner.

References

1. S.M. Kelly, R.B. Brightwell, Software Architecture of the Light Weight Kernel, Catamount, in *Cray User Group*, CUG, 2005
2. Kitten Light Weight Kernel, Sandia National Laboratories. Available https://software.sandia.gov/trac/kitten
3. J.H. Laros III, A Software and Hardware Architecture for a Modular, Portable, Extensible Reliability Availability and Serviceability System, in *IEEE Proceedings of the Workshop on High Performance Computing Reliability Issues*, 2006
4. Cielo, Sandia National Laboratories and Los Alamos Laboratory. Available http://www.lanl.gov/orgs/hpc/cielo/
5. R. Ge, X. Feng, K.W. Cameron, Performance-Constrained Distributed DVS Scheduling for Scientific Applications on Power-aware Clusters, in *Proceedings of the International Conference on High Performance Computing, Networking, Storage, and Analysis (SC)*, ACM/IEEE, 2005
6. K.B. Ferreira, R. Brightwell, P.G. Bridges, Characterizing Application Sensitivity to OS Interference Using Kernel-Level Noise Injection, in *Proceedings of the International Conference on High Performance Computing, Networking, Storage, and Analysis (SC)*, ACM/IEEE, 2008
7. F. Petrini, D. Kerbyson, S. Pakin, The Case of the Missing Supercomputer Performance: Achieving Optimal Performance on the 8,192 Processors of ASCI Q, in *Proceedings of the International Conference on High Performance Computing, Networking, Storage, and Analysis (SC)*, ACM/IEEE, 2003

Chapter 3
Measuring Power

Abstract The effort expended to measure current draw and voltage are enabling technologies critical to conducting the experiments contained in this book. To date, there has been no other work published that has been based on such large-scale fine-grained in situ measurements of energy on a High Performance Computing (HPC) platform. This chapter contains a discussion of both the hardware and software infrastructure used to conduct our experiments.

3.1 Leveraging the Hardware

The Cray XT architecture contains an integrated Reliability Availability and Serviceability (RAS) system comprised of both hardware and software with the goal of increasing the reliability of the overall platform (see Sect. 2.3). At a very high level, the RAS system is responsible for the control and monitoring of the underlying platform. The separate hardware allocated for the RAS system is intended to ensure the primary purpose of the underlying platform—computation—is affected as little as possible. The distinct, but closely integrated, nature of the RAS system provides an out-of-band path that allows a large variety of monitoring data to be collected.

Unlike typical commodity hardware, the Cray XT3/4/5 node boards provide interfaces that can be exploited to measure component level current draw and voltage. Figure 3.1, depicts the logical board, cage, and cabinet connectivity of important components of the RAS system involved in collecting current and voltage measurements. Each node board has an embedded processor called an L0 or *level 0* (depicted in green). The L0 has the ability (and responsibility) to interface with many on board components. To obtain current and voltage measurements the I2C[1] link between the L0 and the Voltage Regulator Modules (VRM) is enlisted. Note, each node (depicted in blue) has an associated VRM (depicted in orange). The black lines connecting

---

[1] The I2C is one of several two-wire serial bus protocols commonly used for this type of component control and monitoring. SMBus, for example, is another common standard.

J. H. Laros III et al., *Energy-Efficient High Performance Computing*,
SpringerBriefs in Computer Science, DOI: 10.1007/978-1-4471-4492-2_3,
© James H. Laros III 2013

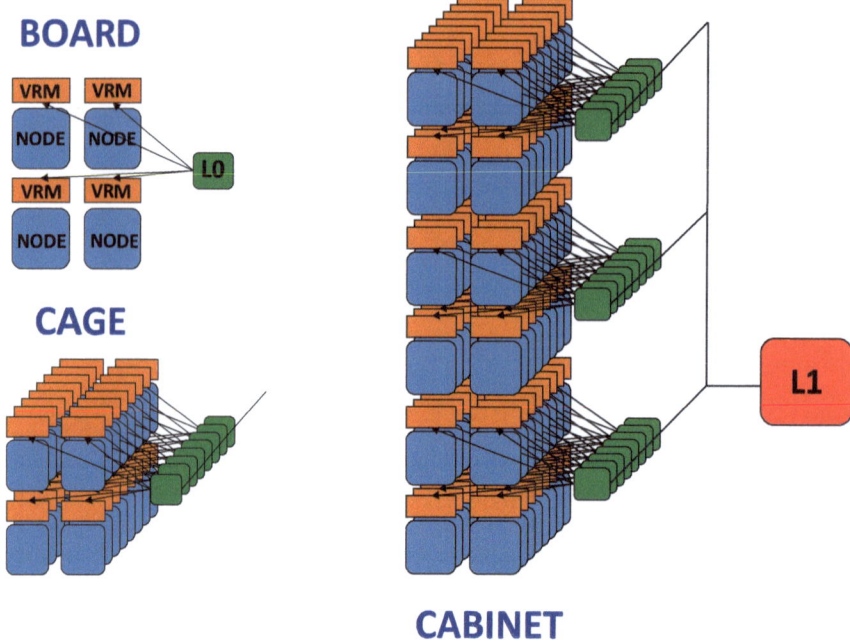

Fig. 3.1 RAS: board, cage and cabinet connectivity

the L0 to each node's VRM represent the I2C interface. In reality, the connectivity is more complicated, involving a number of Peripheral Interface Controllers (PIC micro-controllers) and Field Programmable Gate Arrays (FPGA). The current and voltage measurements are collected by the L0 on each board. In the Cray XT architecture there are eight boards in a cage. Three cages comprise a cabinet. At the cabinet level there is an additional embedded processor called an L1 or *level 1* (depicted in red in Figs. 3.1 and 3.2). Each of the 24 L0s in a cabinet are connected to the cabinet L1 via Ethernet, also depicted by black lines. The L1 acts as a parent for each of the L0s in a cabinet.

Figure 3.2 represents the overall hardware RAS hierarchical topology down to the L0 level. Each cabinet level L1 in the platform connects to the top level System Management Workstation (SMW) (depicted in blue in Fig. 3.2) via Ethernet. Similar to how the L1 acts as a parent for each underlying L0, the SMW acts as a parent for all L1s in the platform. This configuration forms the RAS hardware hierarchy for the Cray XT architecture. This hierarchical configuration provides sufficient scalability for the control and monitoring of very large platforms. To date systems of more than 200 cabinets have been deployed. A 200 cabinet system would be comprised of one top level SMW, 200 L1s and 4800 L0s. The RAS system alone is larger than most commodity clusters. No scalability issues have been encountered during these experiments.

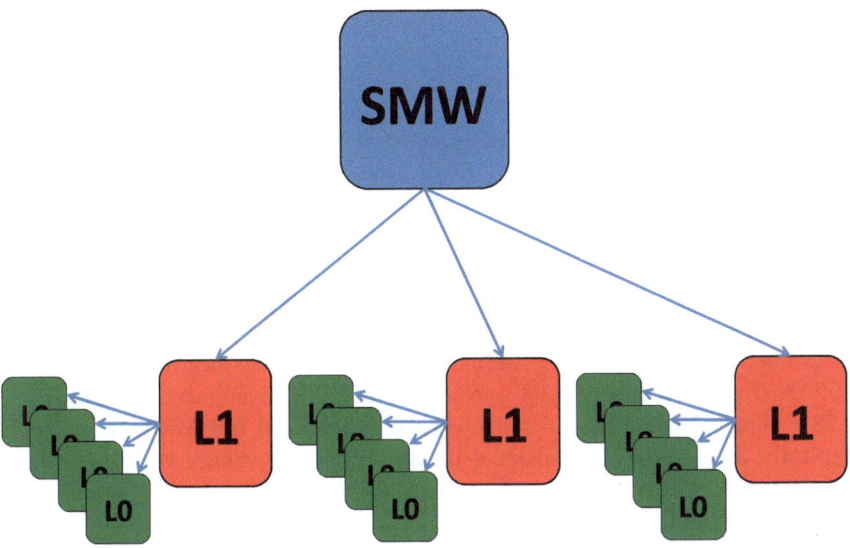

Fig. 3.2 RAS: Hierarchical connectivity

3.2 Software Instrumentation

While the ability to exploit the hardware (collect current and voltage data) is not currently a feature provided by the Cray Reliability availability and serviceability Management System (CRMS), the existing software infrastructure was leveraged in the following way to conduct these experiments.

The CRMS consists of a number of persistent daemons which communicate in a hierarchical manner to provide a wide range of control and monitoring capabilities. The base CRMS software was augmented with a *probing* daemon that runs on each L0 and a single *coalescence* daemon that runs on the top level SMW. The probing daemon registers a callback with the event loop executing in the main L0 daemon process (part of the standard CRMS) to interrogate the VRM at a specific bus: device location (corresponding to each individual node or processor socket). In the standard CRMS, the L0 daemon processes communicate to their parent L1 daemon process (also part of the standard CRMS, executing on the cabinet level L1) through an event router daemon (additionally part of the standard CRMS). In turn, each L1 communicates to the top-level SMW through an event router daemon. The results of a series of timed probes, requested by the probing daemon, are combined at the L0 level and communicated through the standard event router daemon hierarchy to the *coalescence* daemon executing on the SMW, which outputs the results.

The output is a formatted flat file with timestamped hexadecimal current and voltage values for each CPU socket monitored (results are per socket not per core). Figure 3.3 depicts a few sample output lines from an actual experiment. The cname (c14-2c0s3), for example, corresponds to the L0 that resides in the cabinet with

c14-2c0s2,1300491313,n0=0x17,n0_V=0x4fa,n0_W=0x1d, ...,mezz=0x46
c14-2c0s3,1300491313,n0=0x1a,n0_V=0x500,n0_W=0x21, ...,mezz=0x46
c14-2c0s4,1300491313,n0=0x15,n0_V=0x4e3,n0_W=0x1a, ...,mezz=0x46

Fig. 3.3 Sample raw current, voltage, and calculated wattage output data

X coordinate 14, *Y coordinate* 2, cage 0 slot 3. The 2nd field is the timestamp relative to the L0 that collected the data. (Some challenges were encountered when we collected data from L0s with poorly synchronized date and time.) The remaining fields are the current and voltage measurements for this board and a calculated value for power in watts. For example, the entry **n0=0x1a** specifies a current measurement of 26 A. The entry **n0_V=0x500** specifies a voltage measurement of 1,280 mV or 1.28 V. Finally, the calculated wattage value is provided (**n0_W=0x21** or 33 W). Typically, the wattage is calculated using the current and voltage values in the post processing step rather than using the value specified in this output to retain as much precision as possible. The entries shown in Fig. 3.3 omit the values for nodes 1, 2, and 3 in the interest of space. Note, the last field labeled *mezz* represents the Seastar NIC. As can be seen in the samples provided, the current draw is very consistent for the Seastar and does not change in response to load. The power draw for most network interfaces is dominated by the Serializer/Deserializer (SerDes) that drive the high-speed network links. The SerDes typically operate at a constant rate independent of network traffic. One reason for this is to maintain network timing and synchronization. This is one of the challenges of producing tunable networks. While the current draw of the network does not vary over time, it is useful in quantifying the total power used by the node. The measured value from the NIC (Seastar) is used to establish a baseline in the network bandwidth experiments (see Sect. 7.2).

A per socket collection granularity at a frequency of up to 100 samples per second was achieved by leveraging the existing hardware and software foundation of the CRMS. The data used in the experiments contained in this book are at a frequency of one sample per second. Little benefit was found in higher frequency collection for the purposes of this analysis. In addition, we do not have sufficient information concerning the ability of the low-level device to collect discrete values at higher rates. Experiments have verified that samples taken at a rate of one sample per second are discrete measurements. The accuracy of each sample is approximately ±2 A. While the samples are not as accurate as would be optimal, the data remains valuable for comparing deltas. Since the values reported by a single node are consistent, the deltas are very reliable for comparison purposes. This is in contrast with most other platforms where measuring current draw is typically limited to inserting a meter between a power cable and energy source, which results in a very coarse measurement capability at best. The current draw measurements include memory controller activity (since the processors used have an on-board memory controller) but not power used by the memory banks themselves. The granularity and frequency of this sampling capability has enabled real power usage to be observed and used in new and powerful ways that will be detailed in the following chapters.

The impact of the instrumentation on the CRMS was closely monitored. Even at 100 samples per second little impact on the L0 was observed. Likewise, no adverse impact to communication between the L0s and L1 devices, or between the L1s and the SMW has been observed. The instrumentation has been tested on up to 15 Cray XT cabinets (1440 nodes) and no scaling issues have been identified.

3.3 Post Processing Measurement Data

In all of the following experiments, current and voltage measurements are collected, simultaneously, from 15 cabinets (1440 nodes), more specifically each node's VRM, at a frequency of one sample per second over the duration of the entire test period to avoid start up and tear down overhead of the collection process. Since a range of applications were executed at various scales, cabinets were targeted in a distributed manner throughout the platform to achieve consistent collection coverage for the applications tested. For example, the CTH application run on 4096 nodes intersected with 960 of the collection nodes (23 % coverage). Similarly, the AMG application run on 1536 nodes intersected with 480 of the collection nodes (31 % coverage). The number of nodes sampled was not limited by the scalability of the collection mechanism but by the available test time on these large-scale platforms.

Post processing begins with ensuring all data samples used are from nodes involved in the specific application run. The data samples are then synchronized with the application execution start and finish timestamps. The resulting file is used as input for a Perl script which accomplishes the vast majority of post processing automatically. The post processing script has a wide range of capabilities used for analyzing input data for a number of purposes. The following describes a typical analysis.

In Fig. 3.3 notice that a single line of data contains information for all four nodes on a board (and the Seastar or mezz). Each line is first parsed into individual node data and stored in a data-structure designed to increase post processing flexibility and efficiency. Each line also contains a timestamp. Each data sample for each node is stored with an associated timestamp value. The trapezoidal rule is used to integrate these values over time, which approximates the energy used over the duration of the application. This value is expressed in joules and calculated for each individual node. In addition to this calculation, a graph is produced for each node over the duration of the data sample. Graphs are typically produced (using gnuplot) of the absolute measurement values in watts on the X axis and time on the Y axis. Alternatively, plots can be produced using the measured values relative to the measured idle current by sampling the current for a small duration of time before launching the application. A number of output graph types and formats can be specified. For the purposes of displaying energy used over the duration of an application run, the gnuplot filled-curves format is most useful for analysis (example graph can be found in Fig. 6.2).

In addition to calculating an energy value and producing a graph for each node represented in the data, a statistics file is also generated that is used as the basis for cumulative, per application analysis. The statistics file contains the energy for each node along with a number of additional statistics including: total energy (sum), the average or mean, median, mode, and the coefficient of variation (CV). This analysis allows large amounts of data to be processed while ensuring the results are valid. The CV is leveraged to ensure the measurements are dependable since the CV is expressed as a percentage, independent of the magnitude of the data samples. For the purposes of this analysis, the differences between complete samples or deltas are the primary focus. Previous experiments have proven this approach to be very reliable and provide a solid foundation for comparison. This process is used to produce the data and graphs that appear throughout this book.

Chapter 4
Applications

Abstract The applications used in the experiments contained in this book were primarily selected based on their importance to the three Department of Energy (DOE) National Nuclear Security Administration (NNSA) nuclear weapons laboratories (Sandia, Los Alamos, and Lawrence Livermore). As part of the procurement of Cielo, (DOE/NNSA's most recent High Performance Computing (HPC) capability platform (2010)) each laboratory in the Tri-Lab complex specified two production scientific computing applications that would be used in the acceptance phase of the procurement of Cielo. These applications are herein referred to as the *6X* applications (due to the requirement they, on average, must perform six times faster on Cielo, not that there are six applications). The 6X applications include: SAGE, CTH, AMG2006, xNOBEL, UMT, and Charon. In addition to the 6X applications LAMMPS, another production DOE application, and two synthetic benchmarks, HPL and Pallas were used. The following sections provide short descriptions of each application.

4.1 High Performance Computing Applications

SAGE [1, 2] SAIC's Adaptive Grid Eulerian hydro-code, is a multidimensional, multi-material, Eulerian hydrodynamics code with adaptive mesh refinement that uses second-order accurate numerical techniques. SAGE represents a large class of production applications at Los Alamos National Laboratory. Both strong and weak scaling inputs were used in our experiments.

CTH [3] is a multi-material, large deformation, strong shock wave, solid mechanics code developed at Sandia National Laboratories. It has models for multiphase, elastic viscoplastic, porous, and explosive materials. Three-dimensional rectangular meshes; two-dimensional rectangular, and cylindrical meshes; and one-dimensional rectilinear, cylindrical, and spherical meshes are available. CTH has adaptive mesh refinement and uses second-order accurate numerical methods to reduce dispersion

J. H. Laros III et al., *Energy-Efficient High Performance Computing*,
SpringerBriefs in Computer Science, DOI: 10.1007/978-1-4471-4492-2_4,
© James H. Laros III 2013

and dissipation and produce accurate, efficient results. For these experiments the test problem used was a 3-D shaped charge simulation discretized to a rectangular mesh.

AMG2006 [4], developed at the Center for Applied Scientific Computing, at Lawrence Livermore National Laboratory, AMG is a parallel algebraic multigrid solver for linear systems arising from problems on unstructured grids. Based on Hypre [5] library functionality, the benchmark, configured for weak scaling on a logical three-dimensional processor grid $px \times py \times pz$, solves the Laplace equations on a global grid of dimension $(px \times 220) \times (py \times 220) \times (pz \times 220)$.

xNOBEL [6], developed at Los Alamos Laboratory, is a one, two, or three dimensional multi-material Eulerian hydrodynamics code used for solving a variety of high deformation flow of materials problems. The *sc301p* shape charge problem in two dimensions in a weakly scaled configuration was used for all experiments.

UMT [7] is a 3D, deterministic, multigroup, photon transport code for unstructured meshes. The transport code solves the first-order form of the steady-state Boltzmann transport equation.

Charon [8], developed at Sandia National Laboratories, is a semiconductor device simulation code. Charon employs the drift-diffusion model, a coupled system of nonlinear partial differential equations that relate the electric potential to the electron and hole concentrations. A fully implicit, fully coupled solution approach is utilized where Newton's method is used to linearize the discretized equations and a multigrid preconditioned iterative solver is used for the sparse linear systems. Charon uses the solvers from the Sandia National Laboratories Trilinos [9] project. The problem used for this study is a 2D steady-state drift-diffusion simulation for a bipolar junction transistor with approximately 31,000° of freedom per MPI rank.

LAMMPS [10, 11] is a classical molecular dynamics code, and an acronym for Large-scale Atomic/Molecular Massively Parallel Simulator. LAMMPS has potentials for soft materials (biomolecules, polymers) and solid-state materials (metals, semiconductors) and coarse grained or mesoscopic systems. It can be used to model atoms or, more generically, as a parallel particle simulator at the atomic, meso, or continuum scale. When run in parallel, LAMMPS uses message passing techniques and a spatial decomposition of the simulation domain.

4.2 Synthetic Benchmarks

Highly parallel computing benchmark (HPL) [12] is the third benchmark in the Linpack Benchmark Report, used as the benchmark for the bi-annual Top500 report [13]. While the value of the benchmark in measuring how a system will perform for *real* applications can be debated, its pervasiveness is unquestionable. The benchmark solves a random dense linear system in double precision arithmetic on a distributed memory system. The HPL benchmark is well understood and recognized as a compute intensive application.

Pallas [14], now called the Intel MPI Benchmark (IMB), successor to Pallas GmbH, is a suite of benchmarks designed to measure the performance of a wide range of important MPI routines. Pallas is communication intensive.

References

1. R. Weaver, M. Gittings, in *Adaptive Mesh Refinement—Theory and Applications*, Massively Parallel Simulations with DOEs ASCI Supercomputers: An Overview of the Los Alamos Crestone Project, (Springer, Berlin, 2005)
2. D.J. Kerbyson, H.J. Alme, A. Hoisie, F. Petrini, H.J. Wasserman, M. Gittings, in *Proceedings of the International Conference on High Performance Computing, Networking, Storage, and Analysis (SC)*, Predictive Performance and Scalability Modeling of a Large-Scale Application, (ACM/IEEE, 2001)
3. E.S. Hertel, Jr., R.L. Bell, M.G. Elrick, A.V. Farnsworth, G.I. Kerley, J.M. Mcglaun, S.V. Petney, S.A. Silling, P.A. Taylor, L. Yarrington, in *Proceedings of the International Symposium on Shock Waves*, CTH: A Software Family for Multi-Dimensional Shock Physics Analysis, NTIS, 1993
4. R.D. Falgout, P.S. Vassilevski, On generalizing the AMG framework. Soc. Ind. Appl. Math. J. Numer. Anal. **42**, 1669–1693 (2003)
5. Hypre, Lawrence Livermore National Laboratory. [Online]. Available: http://acts.nersc.gov/hypre/
6. M. Gittings, R. Weaver, M. Clover, T. Betlach, N. Byrne, R. Coker, E. Dendy, R. Hueckstaedt, K. New, W.R. Oakes, D. Ranta, R. Stefan, The RAGE radiation-hydrodynamic code. J. Comput. Sci. Discov. **1**(1), 015005 (2008)
7. UMT2K, Lawrence Livermore National Laboratory. [Online]. Available:https://asc.llnl.gov/computing_resources/purple/arch-ive/benchmarks/umt/umt1.2.readme.html
8. P.T. Lin, J.N. Shadid, M. Sala, R.S. Tuminaro, G.L. Hennigan, R.J. Hoekstra, Performance of a parallel algebraic multilevel preconditioner for stabilized finite element semiconductor device modeling. J. Comput. Phys. **228**, 6250–6267 (2009)
9. Trilinos, Sandia National Laboratories. [Online]. Available: http://trilinos.sandia.gov/
10. S. Plimpton, Fast parallel algorithms for short-range molecular dynamics. J. Comput. Phys. **117**, 1–19 (1995)
11. LAMMPS, Sandia National Laboratories. [Online]. Available: http://lammps.sandia.gov/index.html
12. J. Dongarra, J. Bunch, C. Moler, G.W. Stewart, in *Technical Report CS-89-85*, High Performance Linpack HPL, (University of Tennessee, Knoxville, 1989)
13. Top 500 Supercomputer Sites. [Online]. Available: http://www.top500.org/
14. PALLAS, Intel. [Online]. Available: http://www.intel.com/cd/software/products/asmo-na/eng/cluster/mpi/219848.htm

Chapter 5
Reducing Power During Idle Cycles

Abstract The Linux™ community has long been concerned with power saving measures, particularly in the mobile computing sector. Linux has been quick to leverage architectural features of microprocessors to reduce power consumption during idle cycles (and under load as we will discuss in Chap. 6) as these features have become commercially available. The High Performance Computing (HPC) community makes use of Linux on many of their platforms, but lightweight kernels (LWKs) are often used to deliver the maximum amount of performance at large scale (Red Storm and Blue Gene, for example). To achieve greater performance at scale, LWKs have a selective feature set when compared to general purpose operating systems like Linux. As a result, LWKs are a prime area for investigating opportunities for power savings, as long as performance is not affected. In the area of idle power usage, Linux serves as an established benchmark. The goal of this first experiment is to match or beat the idle current draw of Linux.

5.1 Operating System Modifications

The measuring capabilities described in Chap. 3 were first leveraged to examine the current draw and voltage of the Catamount LWK during idle cycles. Initial findings were not surprising. As suspected, power use during idle cycles was very high due to Catamount spinning in the equivalent of a tight loop while awaiting new work.

One of the advantages of most LWKs (Catamount is not an exception) is the relative simplicity of the operating system. The last two versions of Catamount (Catamount Virtual Node (CVN) and Catamount N-Way (CNW))[1] support multi-core sockets. The architecture of Catamount is such that there are only two regions the operating system enters during idle cycles. We first addressed the region where cores greater than 0 (in a zero-based numbering scheme) enter during idle (core 0 will be referred to as the *master* core and cores greater than 0 as *slave* cores).

---

[1] The name Catamount [1] will generally be used throughout this book unless the more specific names CVN and CNW are necessary to point out an important distinction.

J. H. Laros III et al., *Energy-Efficient High Performance Computing*,
SpringerBriefs in Computer Science, DOI: 10.1007/978-1-4471-4492-2_5,
© James H. Laros III 2013

Catamount was modified to individually halt *slave* cores when idle and awaken immediately when signaled by the *master* core. Slave cores are signaled prior to an application launch. If no application is executing on a slave core, the core remains idle without interruption. In the new modified state, cores are put into halt during idle periods. The result of this modification was a significant savings in current draw when slave cores are idle.

As the number of cores per socket increase, the savings will likely increase on capability platforms. Capability class applications are typically memory and/or communication bound (these characteristics are leveraged in later experiments to show energy savings during application runtime). Adding more cores, generally, decreases the balance of the platform, magnifying application bottlenecks. For this reason, many scientific HPC applications utilize less than the total number of available cores per node, driven by desires for increased memory capacity, bandwidth, or both. It should be emphasized that each *slave* core enters and returns from the halt state independently, resulting in very granular control on multi and many-core architectures.

After these positive results, the region of the operating system the master core enters during idle was targeted. The master core is interrupted on every timer tick, or ten times per second. On each interrupt the master core returns from halt and if no work is scheduled returns into the halt state. Even with this additional overhead, significant additional energy savings during idle periods was observed. Note, if only one core is used during an application run it executes on the master core. After extensive testing, these modifications were accepted into the production release of Catamount for Red Storm at Sandia Laboratories and also delivered to the Pittsburgh Supercomputing Center [2].

5.2 Results and Analysis

5.2.1 Idle Power: Before and After

Figure 5.1 depicts measurements obtained running three applications (HPL [3], PALLAS [4] and HPCC [5]) on a dual core AMD Opteron Processor[2] using Compute Node Linux (CNL). Figure 5.2, in contrast, illustrates the results obtained when executing the same three applications on the same physical CPU using Catamount. (Experiments compare results using the same exact hardware to limit variability of measured results.)

The most noticeable difference between the two graphs is the idle power wattage. CNL uses approximately 40 W when idle in contrast to Catamount, which uses approximately 10 W (prior to our operating system modifications Catamount used approximately 60 W). Later results obtained on quad core AMD Opteron[3] sock-

---

[2] AMD Opteron 280 AMD Dual-Core Opteron 2.4 GHz 2M Cache Socket 940 OSA280FAA6CB.

[3] AMD Opteron Budapest 2.2 GHz socket AM2.

ets showed nearly identical idle power wattage measurements for both CNL and Catamount[4] (delta within accuracy of measurement). On this particular dual core architecture the instructions MONITOR and MWAIT are not supported. Both instructions are supported on the quad core architecture used in subsequent testing. Linux can be configured to poll, halt, or use MONITOR/MWAIT during idle. It is possible that what is observed in Fig. 5.1 is a polling loop which in Linux is optimized to conserve power. While CNL draws less power than our unmodified Catamount at idle (40 W for CNL vs. 60 W for unmodified Catamount) it is not as optimal as the modified Catamount implementation (10 W). Later observations on the quad core architecture, where CNL and Catamount draw equivalent amounts of power during idle, are likely the result of CNL exploiting MONITOR/MWAIT. The use of MONITOR/MWAIT should produce similar results to using HALT. Regardless, these results demonstrate the valuable ability to observe and contrast using this fine grained measurement ability. These measurements have demonstrated the first stated goal of equaling (and very possibly beating) the idle power savings of Linux.

These results also provide a first look at *Application Power Signatures* (see Sect. 5.2.2). Each application has a characteristic signature. While small differences in the signature can be observed, even when running the same application on a different operating system the signature is easily recognized (as can be observed in Figs. 5.1 and 5.2 between CNL and Catamount).

A few more subtle points should be made. Without the ability to examine power usage in this way Catamount could only be assumed to be inefficient during idle periods. The actual efficiency could not be quantified empirically. Additionally, the effects of the modifications made could not have been easily measured to determine, definitively, when or if we reached our goal. Likewise, when using CNL, we could make the assumption that CNL benefits from power saving features of Linux but without this capability we would not have recognized the difference in power use between the two CPU architectures.

Using the information obtained by conducting these experiments, some simple calculations for a hypothetical system can be made. For the purposes of this calculation the following assumptions are used: a 13,000 node (dual core) system, 80% utilized (20% idle) ignoring downtime. The idle node hours for this system over a year would be:

$$(13,000 \text{ nodes} * 0.2) * (365 \text{ days/year} * 24 \text{ hours/day}) =$$
$$22.776 * 10^6 \text{ node hours/year}$$
(5.1)

If the idle kilowatt hours saved is calculated based on 50 W per node (the delta between the pre-modified Catamount idle wattage and the modified Catamount idle wattage) the result is:

---

[4] CVN was enhanced to support more than two cores, the resulting Catamount version was named CNW. Unless otherwise specified all results shown after Fig. 5.2 were obtained running on CNW.

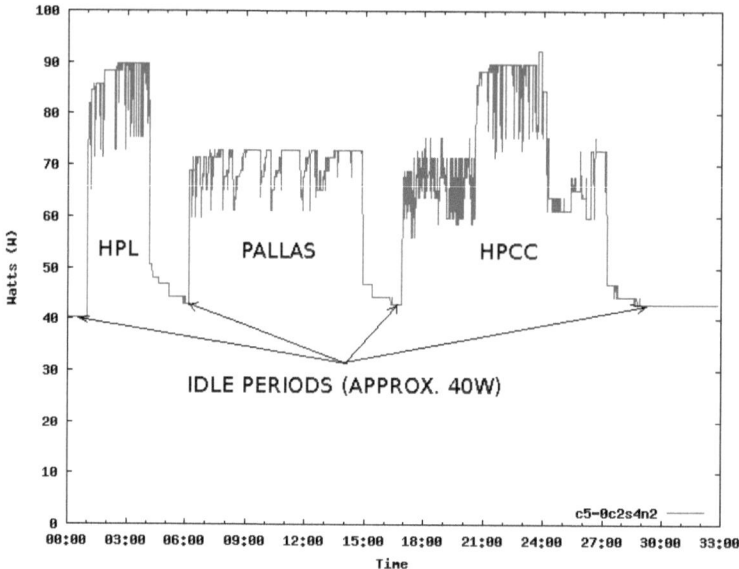

Fig. 5.1 Compute Node Linux (CNL)

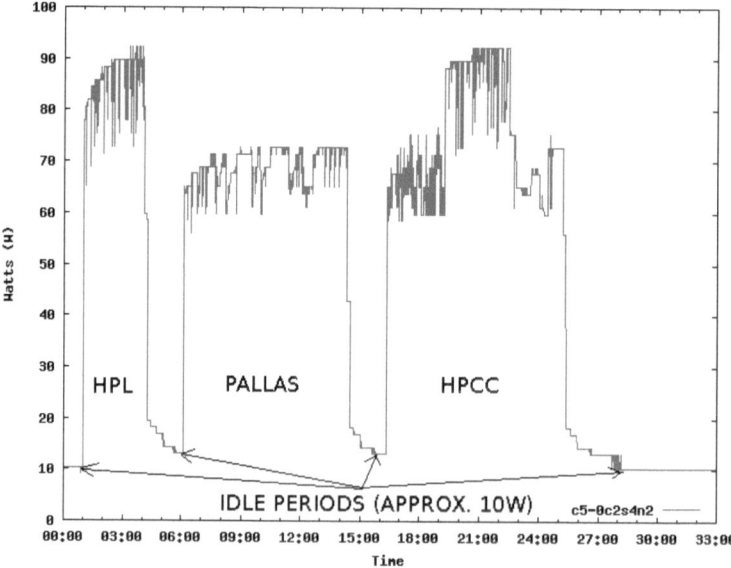

Fig. 5.2 Catamount Virtual Node (CVN)

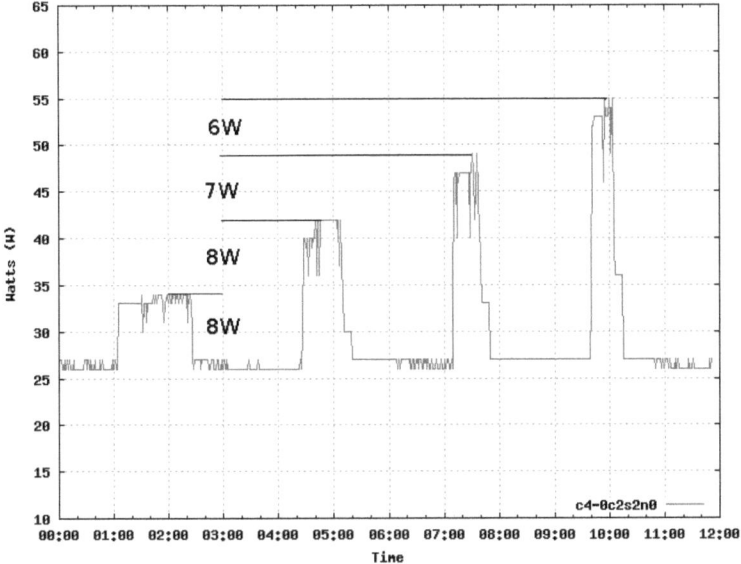

Fig. 5.3 Catamount N-Way per core power utilization

$$(22.776 * 10^6 \text{node hours/year} * 50\text{W/node}) \div 1,000 =$$
$$1.1388 * 10^6 \text{ KW hours/year} \qquad (5.2)$$

Assuming 10 cents/KW hour, based on Department of Energy averages for 2008 [6], the real calculated dollar savings for this hypothetical system is:

$$(1.1388 * 10^6 \text{KW hours/year} * 10 \text{ cents/KW hour}) \div 100 \text{ cents/dollar} =$$
$$113,880 \text{ dollars/year} \qquad (5.3)$$

For a capability system using a figure of 80% utilization as characterized is optimistic. Capability systems are typically intended to support one or more large applications at one time which tends to drive the total resource utilization numbers down. Additionally, this calculation does not consider idle cores resulting from applications that use less than the maximum cores available per node (as previously discussed). In the case of dual core sockets half of the resource could remain idle (in power saving mode) when the system is considered to be 100% utilized. In the case of quad core sockets three-fourths of the resource could potentially remain idle.

Figure 5.3 illustrates incremental power usage on a quad core socket when a short HPL job is executed on one, two, three, and four cores of a quad core node. Even though measurements are on a per node granularity the incremental rise in power usage when additional cores are enlisted can easily be observed. These results provide both a nice illustration of per core savings and a confirmation that the operating system modifications that were applied properly handle per core idle states.

In addition to the previous calculated savings, a 30–40 % additional power savings as a result of not having to remove the additional heat generated by higher idle wattages would be realized. If cooling were included, the cost savings would range from between $148, 044 and $159, 432 per year. By exploiting these power saving measures, significant savings can be realized by targeting idle cores alone.

5.2.2 Application Power Signature

Application Power Signature is the term applied to the measured power usage of an application over the duration of that application. The term signature is used since each application exhibits a repeatable and largely distinct shape when graphed. A user knowledgeable of the application flow can easily distinguish phases of the application simply by viewing the plotted application signature. While simply graphing the resulting data can be useful, the capability is augmented by calculating the energy used over the duration of the application. The result is termed *application energy*. This metric is derived by calculating the area under the application signature curve. To accomplish this the post processing code was enhanced to approximate the definite integral using the trapezoidal rule. The following graphs (Figs. 5.4, 5.5) depict the data collected while running HPCC on Catamount and CNL. HPCC was executed using the same input file on the same physical hardware. Each run used 16 processors (four nodes, four cores per node).

In the upper right hand corner of each graph (Figs. 5.4, 5.5) is the energy used by the application (on a single node, all four cores). Again, notice the similarity of the signatures regardless of the underlying operating system. In this case HPCC finished more quickly on Catamount than CNL. HPCC and other applications have been shown to execute more quickly on Catamount [7]. It is not surprising that an application that takes longer to execute, given similar power draw during execution, will consume more energy. In this case HPCC ran 16 % faster on Catamount. The amount of energy used by HPCC is 13 % less when executed on Catamount versus CNL. HPCC was also tested on quad core nodes using two cores per node (HPCC ran 15 % faster on Catamount and used 13 % less energy) and on dual core nodes using two cores per node (HPCC ran 10 % faster on Catamount and used 10 % less energy). The salient point is that performance is not only important in reducing the runtime of an application but also in increasing the energy efficiency of that application. Additionally, without the ability to examine real power use at this granularity, the energy efficiency of an application could not be quantified.

5.2.3 Power and Noise

Operating system interference, also referred to as noise or jitter, is caused by asynchronous interruption of the application by the system software on the node. Interruptions can be high frequency short duration like the interruption caused by

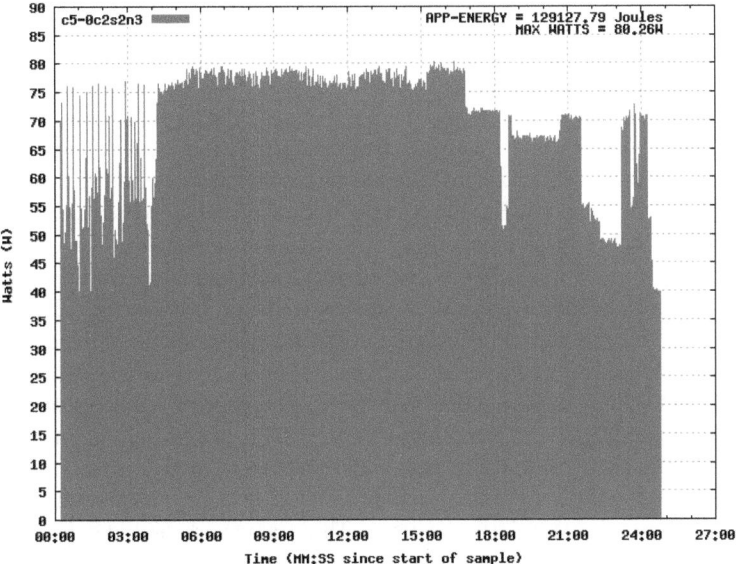

Fig. 5.4 HPCC on Catamount

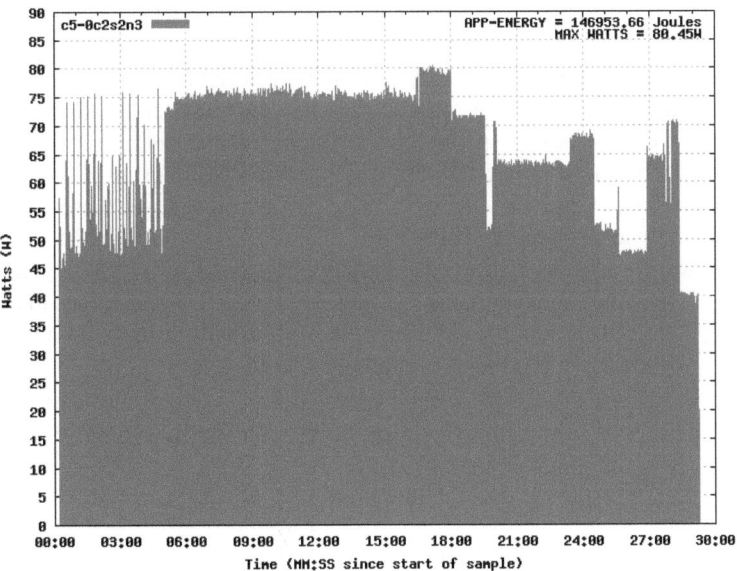

Fig. 5.5 HPCC on CNL

the periodic timer "tick", commonly used by operating systems to keep track of time, to shorter frequency, but relatively longer duration, kernel daemon tasks.

The detrimental side effects of operating system interference on HPC systems have been known and studied, primarily qualitatively, for nearly two decades [8, 9]. Previous investigations have suggested the global performance cost of noise is due to the variance in the time it takes processes to participate in collective operations, such as MPI_Allreduce. LWKs, like Catamount, are essentially noise-less in comparison to general purpose operating systems like Linux. Previous work has shown that operating system noise can have substantial impact on the performance of HPC applications [10]. In addition, this work shows the impact varies by application, some showing relatively no impact in noisy environments while others exhibit exponential slowdowns. While many aspects of the impact of noise on runtime performance are well understood, the impact of noise in terms of energy usage is not. Specifically, the goal of this experiment is to determine if energy usage in noisy environments scales linearly (or otherwise) with the increase in application runtime.

To evaluate the impact of noise, the kernel-level noise injection framework built into the Catamount LWK [10] was used. This framework provides the ability to direct the operating system to inject various per-job noise patterns during application execution. The available parameters for generating the noise pattern include: the frequency of the noise (in Hz), the duration of each individual noise event (in μs), the set of participating nodes, and a randomization method for noise patterns across nodes (not employed for this analysis). The noise is generated (simulated) using a timer interrupt on core 0 of the participating nodes. When the interrupt is generated, Catamount interrupts the application and spins in a tight busy-wait loop for the specified duration. Note, in this case Catamount does not enter halt as described previously. The purpose of specifying the frequency and duration of each noise event separately is to simulate various types of noise that occur on general purpose operating systems. Catamount provides an ideal environment for these studies due to its extremely low native noise signature.

The following analysis focuses on a single application (SAGE). SAGE was chosen based on initial studies and previous analysis done in [10]. Applications like SAGE have the potential to be significantly impacted by noise and any proportional increase in energy. Table 5.1 is a representative sample of the results.

A number of different noise patterns were injected, varying the frequency and duration of the noise. The noise percentage (column one) is determined using Eq. 5.4.

$$((\text{Frequency}(\text{Hz}) * \text{Duration}(\mu s)) \div (1 * 10^6)) * 100 \qquad (5.4)$$

The frequency of the noise (column two) is how often a noise event occurs. The duration (column three) is how long each noise event lasts. The difference in runtime is shown in column four and is relative to the runtime of the application with no noise injected. Likewise, the difference in application energy (column five) is relative to the energy used by the application without noise injected. The results, with the exception of row six, are representative of multiple runs on the same equipment using the same parameters. In addition, the runtime of the application was varied with

Table 5.1 Power Impact of Noise

Noise (%)	Frequency (Hz)	Duration (μs)	Difference in runtime (%)	Difference in application energy (AVG) (%)
2.5	10	2,500	4.0	4.0
1	10	1,000	1.7	1.9
2.5	100	250	2.6	2.5
2.5	1,000	25	2.6	2.5
1	1,000	10	0.1	0.1
10	**10**	**10,000**	**21.6**	**21.0**

consistent results. The results were obtained using 16 quad core nodes. The application utilized core 0 only since noise can only be injected on core 0 using this framework. What was observed is that the difference in application energy used by applications when noise is injected is linearly proportional to the difference in runtime. If the impact of the injected noise is normalized, even in the most extreme example (again excluding row six) the impact of noise on both the runtime and the application energy is approximately 1.5 %. The results were found to be very consistent. The experiment was repeated at a larger scale (48 nodes, again utilizing only core 0) and observed results were consistent with Table 5.1. In an effort to simulate effects seen at larger scale a large amount of noise (10 %) was introduced while running the same application. The results (row six of Table 5.1) show a larger impact to both runtime and application energy (approximately 11 % when normalized). These results are significant in the fact that they show the same linearly proportional increase in application energy for applications effected by noise. Though Table 5.1 shows small percentage increases in runtime for various noise patterns, accompanied by proportional increases in the percentage of energy used, these results were obtained at a relatively small scale. The runtime of some applications can increase dramatically at larger scale in noisy environments.

In Fig. 5.6, the measured slowdown of POP, CTH, and SAGE, at scale, is observed. In this figure the Y-axis is the global accumulation of noise for the application. The global accumulation is computed by taking the slowdown of the app in a noisy environment versus a baseline with no OS noise and subtract the amount of locally injected noise. For example, if a 2.5 % net processor noise signature is injected, a 20 % slowdown is measured and the global accumulation of noise would be 17.5 %. As seen in Fig. 5.6 with only 2.5 % net processor noise injected the slowdown for POP exceeds 1,200 % at scale. A proportional increase of 1,200 % application energy at scale can therefore be projected. The inset of Fig. 5.6 also shows considerable slowdowns for SAGE and CTH due to noise. While not as dramatic as POP, the additional impact on application energy projected by our analysis is proportionally as significant.

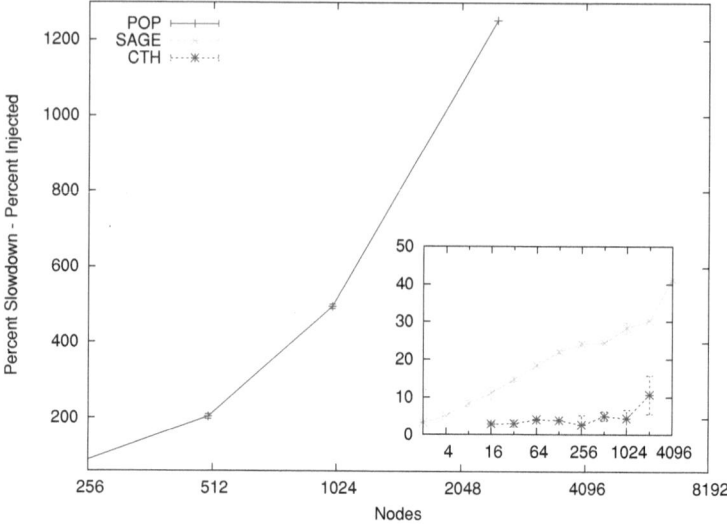

Fig. 5.6 Slowdown as a result of noise measured at scale from [10]

References

1. S.M. Kelly, R.B. Brightwell, Software architecture of the light weight kernel, Catamount, in *Cray User Group*, (CUG), 2005
2. Pittsburgh Supercomputing Center, http://www.psc.edu
3. J. Dongarra, J. Bunch, C. Moler, G.W. Stewart, High Performance Linpack HPL, in *Technical Report CS-89-85*, University of Tennessee, 1989
4. PALLAS, Intel, Available: http://www.intel.com/cd/software/products/asmo-na/eng/cluster/mpi/219848.htm
5. HPCC, DARPA, Available: http://icl.cs.utk.edu/hpcc/
6. DOE Energy Statistics, Department of Energy, http://www.eia.doe.gov/cneaf/electricity/epm/table5_6_a.html
7. C.T. Vaughan, J.P. VanDyke, S.M. Kelly, Application performance under different XT operating systems, in *Cray User Group*, (CUG), 2008
8. R. Zajcew, P. Roy, D. Black, C. Peak, P. Guedes, B. Kemp, J. LoVerso, M. Leibensperger, M. Barnett, F. Rabii, D. Netterwala, An OSF/1 UNIX for Massively Parallel Multicomputers, in *Proceedings of the USENIX Technical Conference*, USENIX, 1993
9. F. Petrini, D. Kerbyson, S. Pakin, The Case of the missing supercomputer performance: achieving optimal performance on the 8,192 Processors of ASCI Q, in *Proceedings of the International Conference on High Performance Computing, Networking, Storage, and Analysis (SC)*, ACM/IEEE, 2003
10. K.B. Ferreira, R. Brightwell, P.G. Bridges, Characterizing application sensitivity to OS interference using kernel-level noise injection, in *Proceedings of the International Conference on High Performance Computing, Networking, Storage, and Analysis (SC)*, ACM/IEEE, 2008

Chapter 6
Tuning CPU Power During Application Runtime

Abstract In Chap. 5, the focus was on reducing power by exploiting idle cycles. In the experiments outlined in this chapter and in Chap. 7 the focus is on identifying opportunities to reduce the energy use of a running application without affecting performance. As mentioned previously, determining what is, and is not, an acceptable trade-off between energy and performance is somewhat subjective. The motivation of the following experiments is to show that significant energy savings can be achieved by tuning architectural components, specifically the CPU, on a per application basis during execution.

6.1 Static CPU Frequency Tuning

Typical approaches employed by operating systems, such as Linux, while efficient for single server or laptop implementations, have proven to be detrimental when used at scale causing the equivalent of operating system jitter [1]. For this reason, most, if not all, sites that deploy clusters at medium to large scale disable these features while running applications (some sites enable these features during idle cycles). It is clear that techniques designed for laptop energy efficiency are not directly applicable to large-scale High Performance Computing (HPC) platforms. In the following CPU frequency scaling experiments, a more deterministic approach is taken which ensures all cores participating in an application are operating at the target frequency in lock step. This is termed *static* frequency modification. First, the runtime impact is contrasted with the energy savings on a per application basis. This analysis focuses on CPU energy. In Chap. 7, the runtime impact is contrasted with total system energy while tuning the network interface, again on a per application basis. Both approaches provide valuable insight.

Feng [2] reports that the CPU is the largest single consumer of energy on a node. While Feng's analysis is for a commodity board that contains disk and other components, a similar analysis can be performed on the hardware used for these

J. H. Laros III et al., *Energy-Efficient High Performance Computing*,
SpringerBriefs in Computer Science, DOI: 10.1007/978-1-4471-4492-2_6,
© James H. Laros III 2013

experiments. A Cray XT architecture node board contains only CPU, memory, and a Network Interface Controller (NIC).[1] If 20 W is allowed for memory, 25 W for the NIC (based on the measured value) and a measured value for CPU based on the data collected for these experiments, the CPU ranges from 44 to 57 % of the total node power. Clearly, since the CPU is the largest consumer of power, it is productive to analyze it both in isolation and as a component of total system power. In the following experiment CPU data is measured in isolation.

6.1.1 Operating System Modifications

A number of targeted modifications were made to Catamount to accomplish these experiments. First, it was necessary to interrogate chip architecture capabilities to determine if Advanced Power Management (APM) is supported. More specifically, the CPU is interrogated to determine if hardware P-state control is supported. P-states, or performance states, are predetermined frequency and voltage settings supported by the particular processor architecture. The architecture used for these experiments supports up to five P-states numbered 0–4. Higher numbered P-states generally represent lower frequency (performance) and lower power. Even if APM is enabled, however, only a single P-state is required to be defined. In addition, even if multiple P-states are defined, they may have identical definitions. This is typically not the case but enforces the importance of closely interrogating specific hardware capabilities, and dynamically adjusting to them. Changing P-states requires writing to P-state related Model Specific Register (MSR). If APM is not supported, writing to P-state MSRs is fatal. From this point forward it is assumed APM is supported, multiple P-states are defined, and at least two P-states define different operating frequencies and voltages.

The method of frequency scaling used in these experiments is currently limited to frequencies defined in the P-state table, although most processors support frequency stepping in 100 MHz increments. The impetus of changing frequency is ultimately to lower the input voltage to the processor. Power is proportional to the frequency, capacitance, and voltage squared. By this definition the largest impact on power can be obtained by lowering the input voltage. Both the processor and the infrastructure must support dynamic voltage transitions to take advantage of this potential power savings. While it is unlikely that future architectures will support independent per core power planes, there will likely be multiple power domains per processor chip. Understanding how these power planes are partitioned (which cores are on which planes) will be important to achieve maximum energy savings while maintaining performance. On the test platforms used for these experiments all cores were required to be in the same *higher* P-state before a lower input voltage could be achieved. Basically, if one core is operating at a higher frequency (which requires a higher

---

[1] The small amount of power used by the embedded controller is not included since it would be amortized across the four nodes present on the board and be largely insignificant for this purpose.

Table 6.1 Test platform P-states, CPU frequencies and input voltages

P-state	CPU Frequency		Input Voltage	
	Red Storm(GHz)	Jaguar(GHz)	Red Storm(V)	Jaguar(V)
0	2.2	2.1	1.200	1.200
1	2.0	2.1	1.200	1.200
2	1.7	1.7	1.150	1.150
3	1.4	1.4	1.075	1.075
4	1.1	1.1	1.050	1.050

input voltage) the input voltage to the processor remains at the voltage necessary to support the highest active frequency [current lowest active core P-state or Current Operating Frequency (COF)]. While describing the subtleties of serial and parallel voltage planes is beyond the scope of this book, they are important architectural details and cannot be overlooked in practice.

At a very early stage in the boot process the default P-state and supported P-states of each core are collected. This information is stored and used by a trap function added to handle a variety of P-state related functionality. Since changing P-states is a privileged call (writing to MSRs) the ability to change P-states was added in two parts; an operating system trap and a user level library interface. The trap implements query functionality to determine what P-states are available, what P-state the core is presently in and of course the ability to transition from the current P-state to an alternate supported P-state. The trap also reports the final P-state achieved and in debug mode the number of nanoseconds the P-state transition took. The amount of time necessary to transition between P-states is not important for the experiments covered in this book since a single static change prior to application execution is accomplished. Transition time becomes a critical consideration when more dynamic methods of CPU frequency scaling are employed.

Table 6.1 lists the supported P-states, corresponding CPU frequencies and required input voltages from both Red Storm and Jaguar. Note that the default P-state on Red Storm is P-state 0. Testing was conducted on P-states 0, 2, 3, and 4 on Red Storm. On Jaguar the default P-state is P-state 1. Testing on Jaguar was conducted using P-states 1, 2, 3 and 4. Some inconsistency was observed in the reported P-state *vids* (core voltage ID) on Jaguar. Since both the current and the voltage were directly measured, these inconsistencies had no affect on the results (actual measured values are used).

The frequency in MHz at the end of each entry is calculated using the CPU *fid* (core frequency ID) and the (core divisor ID) CPU *did* (see BKDG [3] for additional information). Among the additional information contained in a P-state entry is the CPU *vid*, which specifies the necessary input voltage to support the operating frequency of the P-state and the (north-bridge voltage ID) *nbvid*, voltage necessary to support the north-bridge. For the architecture used in these experiments the nbvid in each case is the same as the vid.

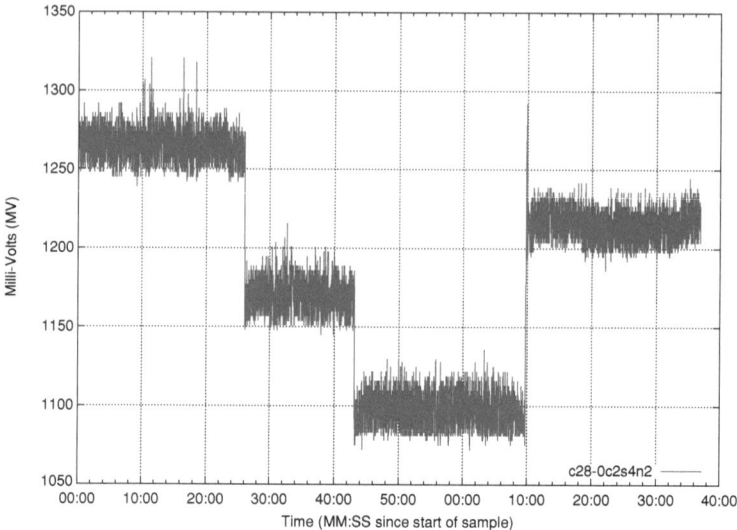

Fig. 6.1 Input voltage drop in response to P-state frequency changes

The input voltage, represented in hexadecimal, can be found in the BKDG for the processor family. The 10th family supports both a parallel and a serial voltage interface. The platforms employed in these experiments use the serial voltage interface infrastructure. A vid of 0x1c corresponds to 1.200 V.[2] By selecting P-state 2 the input voltage can be lowered to vid 0x20 (1.150 V). In this example notice the *vids* for P-state 0 and P-state 1 are identical. Using P-state 1 offers little advantage since the operating frequency (fid) is lowered with no accompanying reduction in voltage.

Figure 6.1 displays the measured voltage changes (on Jaguar) when the P-state is altered through the following states: P-state 0, P-state 2, P-state 3, P-state 1. Note, a difference was observed in the input voltage between P-state 0 and P-state 1. While the P-state table (Table 6.1) indicates that both P-state 0 and P-state 1 should operate at 1.200 V, we see that P-state 0 is operating, at least on this node, at 1.250 V. It is due to anomalies such as this that we feel it is important to measure actual values.

The current implementation of the operating system trap has proven to be extremely stable. Transition between P-states is accomplished in a step-wise fashion. If, for example, P-state 4 is requested and the core is currently in P-state 0, the transition occurs between P-states 0 and 4 one by one. This approach was found to be more reliable than directly requesting cores to transition to specific P-states. Additionally, the transition time does not impact the results, at least in the case of static P-state operation. This method will have to be revisited for dynamic frequency scaling experiments since it is likely to incur too much overhead.

---

[2] To determine the voltage the hexadecimal value must first be converted to its binary representation, then referenced in the appropriate table for either serial or parallel power planes in the BKDG [3].

To confirm that P-state transitions are successful the ability to monitor both current draw and voltage on a per socket granularity is employed. After requesting a change in P-state a corresponding drop in input voltage can be observed (see Fig. 6.1). Note, in some cases, even when the transition to a new lower voltage P-state has been confirmed (recorded in the MSR), a drop in input voltage does not occur (verified through measurement). While this is suboptimal, it has the effect of understating the results of these experiments since energy is calculated based on measured voltages. In other words, if all transitions behaved ideally, the energy savings would be greater than reported in the results.

More issues were observed, in general, while running on Red Storm than on Jaguar. Further investigation led to the discovery that while Jaguar has very recent Peripheral Interface Controller (PIC) firmware revisions, Red Storm's PIC revisions are quite dated. This is partially due to the age of Red Storm. Since Red Storm was serial number one of this architecture, PIC updates were expected to be infrequent therefore remote update capability was not incorporated into the platform. Benefiting from the lessons learned from earlier installations, the hardware used on Jaguar does support remote PIC updates and therefore it is much less intrusive to keep PIC firmware up to date. Obtaining results for these experiments proved much less problematic on Jaguar likely due to the up-to-date PIC firmware which affects many of the hardware characteristics we manipulate.

6.1.2 Library Interface

Since changing P-states (changing COF and potentially input voltage) is a privileged operation, the trap is accessed through a variety of functions provided by a user level library. While a single trap function implements all of the frequency change functionality, for ease of use and clarity a library function interface is implemented to exploit each capability individually.

1. **cpu_pstates(void)**—returns detailed processor P-state information
2. **cpu_freq_step(P-state)**—request a P-state transition (up or down)
3. **cpu_freq_default(void)**—returns default processor P-state

In this experiment, the affects of CPU frequency modification are quantified. Prior to executing the user application a *control* application is executed. The control application simply changes the CPU's COF by changing the CPU's P-state to the desired level [cpu_freq_step(P-state)]. The control application is launched on every core of each CPU that will be used in the test application. Note, while convenient for these experiments, a separate control application would not be required in a production environment. For example, a user environment variable could be defined and used by the runtime, or a flag could be specified at launch time. Clearly, there are many ways to enable this capability. P-state changes are accessible from any portion of the software stack using this library interface.

Following execution of the control application the HPC application under test is executed on the same nodes. The HPC application will run at a lower frequency defined by the P-state selected using the control program. During the execution of the HPC application data is collected for both current draw and voltage at one second intervals. Once the HPC application is completed all nodes are returned to the default P-state or a new P-state is selected for a subsequent experiment with cpu_freq_step(P-state).

The trap and library interface was designed to support both static and dynamic frequency scaling. Initially, it was assumed that it would be necessary to change frequency often during application execution to achieve an acceptable trade-off between performance and energy. During testing, it was discovered that large benefits exist for static frequency scaling. Static frequency scaling has many benefits including simplicity and stability.

6.2 Results and Analysis: CPU Frequency Tuning

The following discussion refers to Table 6.2 and Figs. 6.2 and 6.3. Increases in runtime or energy percentage in Table 6.2 are indicated by positive numbers. Negative values or decreases are indicated by parenthesized numbers (all relative to the baseline values listed). In all cases, care was taken to use the same nodes for each application execution. Figures 6.2 and 6.3 were created by overlaying the energy results from an individual node for P-states 1–4 running the specified application.

The frequency scaling experiments were conducted during five separate dedicated systems times. Four of the experiments were conducted on Jaguar during eight to twelve-hour sessions. The final experiments were conducted on Red Storm during a three-day dedicated system time. Over this period a range of experiments were conducted using both real production scientific applications and synthetic benchmarks listed and described in Chap. 4. As can be seen in Table 6.2 some applications were tested in all available P-states. Other applications exhibited clear results in early testing and did not warrant further experiments. In some cases, results at higher P-states (lower frequencies) were not obtained primarily due to hardware issues (namely PIC revision issues as previously described).

Decreasing CPU frequency, in general, will slow active computation. If applications were solely gated by computation this approach would be entirely detrimental. However, applications exhibit a range of characteristics. In this experiment, the CPU frequency is altered and the impact on energy and runtime is measured (other platform parameters are left unchanged). The extremes, or bounds, are represented by two synthetic benchmarks, HPL and Pallas. Note, for all experiments both runtime and energy are contrasted to the baseline runs conducted at P-states 0 or 1 (depending on the platform used) and reported as percent increase or decrease from the baseline value in Table 6.2. For the baseline runs the execution time in seconds (s) and the energy used in Joules (J) is recorded. The CPU frequency experiments focused on the effect that CPU frequency modifications had on CPU energy alone. In [2] Feng eval-

Table 6.2 Experiment #1: CPU frequency scaling: run-time and CPU energy %difference versus Baseline

	Nodes/cores	Baseline frequency		P-2 - 1.7 GHz %Diff		P-3 - 1.4 GHz %Diff		P-4 - 1.1 GHz %Diff	
		Run-time (s)	Energy (J)	Run-time	Energy	Run-time	Energy	Run-time	Energy
HPL	6000/24000	1571	4.49×10^8	21.1	(26.4)				
Pallas	1024/1024	6816	1.72×10^8	2.30	(43.6)				
AMG2006	1536/6144	174	9.49×10^6	7.47	(32.0)	18.4	(57.1)	39.1	(78.0)
LAMMPS	4096/16384	172	2.79×10^7	16.3	(22.9)	36.0	(48.4)	69.8	(72.2)
SAGE (weak)	4096/16384	249	4.85×10^7	0.402	(39.5)				
SAGE (weak)	1024/4096	337	1.51×10^7	3.86	(38.9)	7.72	(49.9)		
CTH	4096/16384	1753	3.60×10^8	14.4	(28.2)	29.0	(38.9)		
xNOBEL	1536/6144	542	4.96×10^7	6.09	(35.5)	11.8	(50.3)		
UMT	4096/16384	1831	3.48×10^8	18.0	(26.5)				
Charon	1024/4096	879	4.47×10^7	19.1	(27.8)				

uates CPU power as a percentage of total system power both during idle cycles and under application load. Even at idle, the CPU accounts for 14 % of the total power draw according to their measurements. More significant to this research, Feng's measurements suggest that during load the CPU accounts for more than a third (35 %) of the total node power draw. As previously stated, on the platforms used in these experiments the CPU accounts for between 44 and 57 % of total node energy. We recognize that additional runtime will be accompanied by additional energy use from other node components, such as memory and network. These additional factors will be accounted for in our next study that takes a broader look at total system energy. Evaluating both CPU power in isolation and as part of total system power provides important insights.

HPL is largely a compute intensive application. HPL was chosen to demonstrate an application that should be highly impacted by reducing CPU frequency. HPL results were as expected. In Table 6.2 it is observed that a change to P-state 2 causes a 21.1 % increase in run-time and a 26.4 % decrease in energy used. This would likely not be an acceptable trade-off for a real application unless the priority was energy savings.

In contrast to HPL, Pallas (IMB) is a highly communication intensive benchmark. Pallas was chosen to demonstrate an application that would be, potentially, less affected by reductions in CPU frequency. Again, as expected, Pallas demonstrates only a 2.30 % increase in run-time and a 43.6 % reduction in energy used when run in P-state 2. This would certainly be a favorable trade-off for most, if not all, applications. Given the results from these synthetic benchmarks, it is expected that real applications will fall somewhere in between these two extremes. Applications are addressed in table order.

Results for AMG2006 at P-states 1–4 at a scale of 6 K cores were obtained. At P-state 2 an increase in run-time of 7.47 % was observed, accompanied by an energy savings of 32.0 %. Note, the longest of three runtimes was used in each case for the final measurements. AMG2006 had a short runtime and it was observed that the shortest runtime in P-state 2 was actually faster than the longest runtime in P-state 1. It is, therefore, clear that AMG2006 could benefit from a reduction in frequency to, at a minimum, P-state 2. The trade-off at P-state 3 is not as clear. The runtime impact is proportionally greater than the energy savings at P-states 3 and 4. Note, while P-state 4 exhibits a significant hit in run-time the largest savings in energy recorded in these experiments was observed. Depending on policies and/or priorities AMG2006 might be able to take advantage of any of the available P-states to produce significant savings in energy.

LAMMPS (tested at 16 K cores), in contrast to AMG2006, does not display a clear win when run at lower frequencies. Results at P-state 2 show a 16.3 % increase in run-time and a 22.9 % decrease in energy. Not a clear win but in some cases this might be an acceptable trade-off. The results for P-states 3 and 4 demonstrate a significant hit in runtime. Increases in runtime of this magnitude might not be acceptable in an HPC environment, but LAMMPS does, however, show a correspondingly large savings in energy at P-states 3 and 4. Again, this may be acceptable in some circumstances

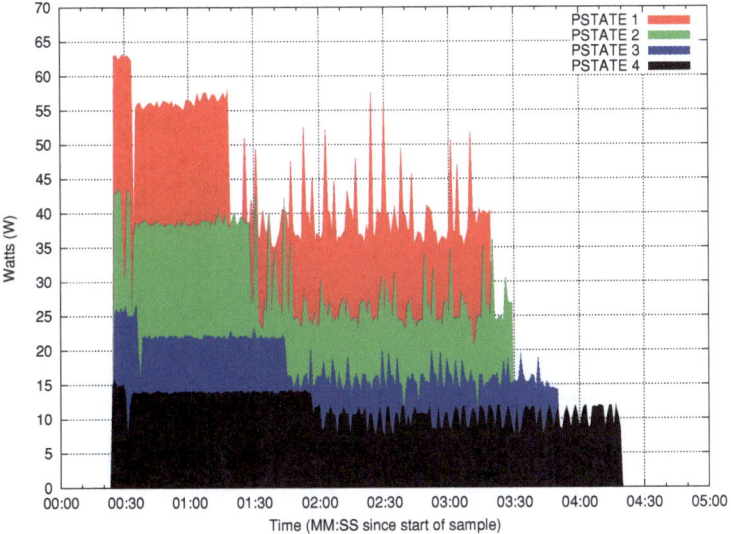

Fig. 6.2   AMG executed at P-states 1–4

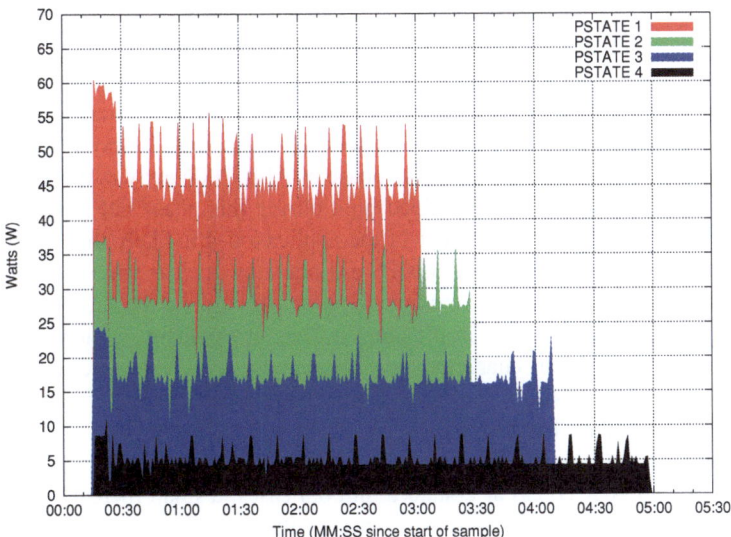

Fig. 6.3   LAMMPS executed at P-states 1–4

where energy consumption is the primary consideration or policy decisions enforce energy limitations.

Figures 6.2 and 6.3 graphically depict each of the four executions of AMG2006 and LAMMPS at P-states 1–4. The shaded area under each curve represents the energy used over the duration of the application. Figure 6.2 clearly depicts the posi-

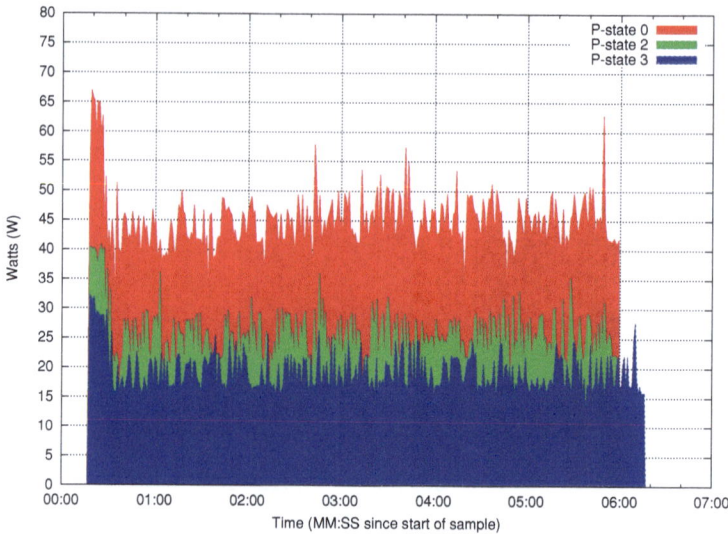

Fig. 6.4 SAGE executed at P-states 0,2 and 3

tive runtime versus energy trade-off (for AMG2006) indicated in Table 6.2 especially between P-states 1 and 2. In contrast, more dramatic increases in runtime can be seen in Fig. 6.3 for LAMMPS. While AMG2006 showed a favorable trade-off between runtime and energy when run at lower frequencies there might be even more benefit to obtain. Notice the compute intensive phase of AMG2006 early in the application execution. If CPU frequency remained high during this phase but transitioned to a lower frequency for the remainder of the application it is likely that the benefits would be even greater. While LAMMPS did not show a clear win when lowering CPU frequency, notice the regular compute phases throughout the entire application execution (indicated by peaks in the graph). Chapter 9 contains a short discussion of how these application characteristics, once understood, could be leveraged to obtain power savings even in applications that do not present a clear choice when we statically modify the CPU frequency.

Results for SAGE were obtained using a weak scaling problem at two different scales (4 K and 16 K cores) at P-state 2. In both cases, a small increase in runtime (0.402 % at 16 K and 3.86 % at 4 K) is observed with a significant reduction in energy (39.5 % at 16 K and 38.9 % at 4 K). Results for a 4 K core run of SAGE at P-state 3 were also obtained. The impact on runtime almost doubled but remains low while some additional energy savings were recorded. Based on these observations, it is possible that the 16 K core SAGE would also demonstrate a favorable trade-off at P-state 3. Figure 6.4 provides the best illustration of energy savings versus runtime impact. The difference in the area under the curves (energy used in joules) between P-states 0 and 2 is evident while the difference in run-time is indistinguishable.

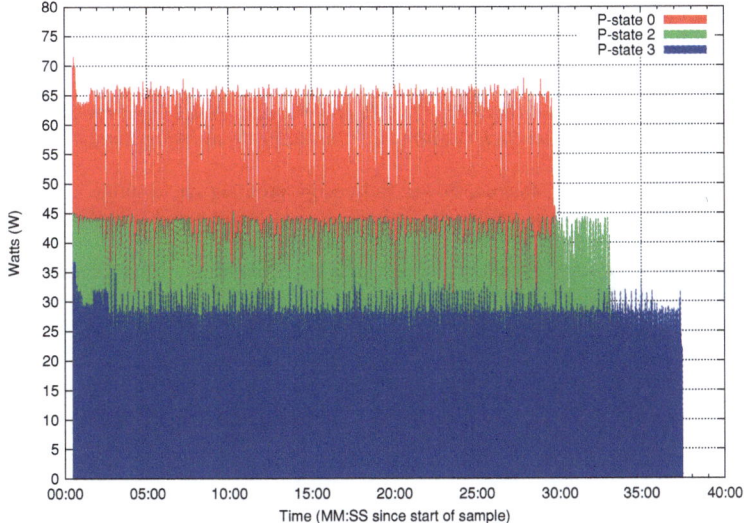

Fig. 6.5 CTH executed at P-states 0,2 and 3

CTH was executed at P-states 0, 2 and 3 at a scale of 16 K cores. Similar to LAMMPS, there is no clear win with CTH when the CPU frequency is lowered. Figure 6.5 graphically illustrates a large runtime impact versus energy savings between P-states. Also, like LAMMPS, CTH has regular compute and communication phases, but phase transitions are much more frequent, as can be seen in Fig. 6.5. LAMMPS and CTH will likely be the targets of future experiments in dynamic CPU frequency scaling at large scale.

Results for xNOBEL at 6 K cores at P-states 0, 2 and 3 were obtained. The results indicate that xNOBEL, like AMG2006, is a good candidate for CPU frequency reduction, even using this static method. Having the ability to tune CPU frequency at large scale for this application would be a clear win.

UMT and Charon behaved in a similar manner. Since UMT was run at a much larger scale than Charon (16 K cores vs. 4 K cores) the results obtained for UMT are more meaningful and more accurately represent what could be expected at large scale. Charon may act differently when run at larger scale but these results indicate that both UMT and Charon are sensitive to CPU frequency changes. It is possible that further analysis will reveal opportunities to dynamically scale frequency during the execution of these applications.

The CPU is only one component that affects application performance. In the following chapter, network bandwidth tuning is applied and the resulting performance versus total system energy trade-off is evaluated.

References

1. F. Petrini, D. Kerbyson, S. Pakin The case of the missing supercomputer performance: Achieving Optimal Performance on the 8,192 processors of ASCI Q. in *Proceedings of the International Conference on High Performance Computing, Networking, Storage, and Analysis (SC)*, ACM/IEEE, 2003
2. X. Feng, R. Ge, K. W. Cameron, Power and energy profiling on scientific applications on distributed systems, in *Proceedings of the International Parallel and Distributed Processing Symposium (IPDPS)*, IEEE, 2005
3. BKDG: AMD BIOS and Kernel Developers Guide for AMD Family 10h Processors Rev 3.48, Advanced Micro Devices. http://www.amd.com

Chapter 7
Network Bandwidth Tuning During Application Runtime

Abstract Chapter 6 showed the effects that CPU frequency tuning had on application energy and performance. In this chapter, we will evaluate the impact that tuning the network bandwidth has on energy and performance of real scientific computing applications running at large scale. This analysis will evaluate the impact on total node energy, in contrast to the CPU frequency tuning experiments that focused on CPU energy. These experiments provide further evidence that tuning components on large-scale High Performance Computing (HPC) platforms can result in significant energy savings.

7.1 Enabling Bandwidth Tuning

The goal of the experiments described in this chapter was to determine the effect on runtime performance and energy of production scientific applications run at very large scale while tuning the network bandwidth of an otherwise balanced platform [1]. To accomplish network bandwidth scaling two different tunable characteristics of the Cray XT platform were leveraged. First, the interconnect bandwidth of the Seastar was tuned to reduce the network bandwidth in stages to 1/2 and 1/4th of full bandwidth. Since the network bandwidth could not be reduced further by tuning the Seastar, the injection bandwidth was tuned, effectively reducing the network bandwidth to 1/8th speed. This allowed for the most accurate stepwise reduction in overall network bandwidth that could be achieved, using this architecture, and a more complete analysis of the effects of network bandwidth tuning on energy.

Modifying the network interconnect bandwidth on the Cray XT3 (or any XT platform using Seastar) requires a fairly simple change to the router configuration file which is consulted (if present) during the routing process of the boot sequence. This unfortunately necessitates a full system reboot for every alteration of the interconnect bandwidth. Typically, all four rails of the Seastar are configured on. This is the default behavior but the number of rails can also be specified in the *rail_enable* field of the

J. H. Laros III et al., *Energy-Efficient High Performance Computing*,
SpringerBriefs in Computer Science, DOI: 10.1007/978-1-4471-4492-2_7,
© James H. Laros III 2013

router configuration file by specifying a single hex number (representing the four configuration bits[1]). In the following experiments, the interconnect bandwidth of the Seastar was configured to effectively tune the network bandwidth to full (baseline), 1/2, and 1/4th speed.

Since the interconnect bandwidth on the XT architecture is far greater than the injection bandwidth of an individual node, the interconnect bandwidth had to be reduced to 1/2 before it produced a measurable effect from the perspective of a single node. It is important to note, the interconnect topology of this platform (Red Storm) is a modified mesh (mesh in x and y directions, torus in z direction). Multiple nodes may route through an individual Seastar depending on communication patterns and where they logically reside in the network topology. For this reason, the experiments were limited to one application execution at a time. This allowed for the nearest estimation of the impact of network bandwidth tuning on an individual application. Running other applications concurrently would be an interesting experiment but would greatly complicate analysis and was beyond the scope of this experiment (and the available resource time).

Tuning the node injection bandwidth, to further reduce the network bandwidth, requires a small modification to the Cray XT bootstrap source code. Cray provided access to this source code under a proprietary license. The portion of the code that required modification (*coldstart*) serves an equivalent purpose to the BIOS on a personal computer or server. Early in the power-on sequence, coldstart initializes the HyperTransport (HT) link that connects each node to its dedicated SeaStar network interface. The speed of this link (Bandwidth (BW) in Bytes/second) is determined by its operating frequency (S) and width in bits (B):

$$S \text{ clocks/sec} \times 2 \text{ bits/clock/wire} \times B \text{ wires} \times 1\text{Byte/8bits} = BW \qquad (7.1)$$

In normal operation, the injection bandwidth is determined by the maximum negotiated rate between the node and the Seastar. Similar to modification of the interconnect bandwidth, a reboot is required to configure the injection bandwidth to the desired setting. Normally, the links operate at $S = 800\,\text{MHz}$ and utilize the full $B = 16$ bits of each link resulting in an injection bandwidth of 3.2 GB/s (Eq. 7.1). To achieve 1/8th injection bandwidth each link is configured to run at $S = 200\,\text{MHz}$ with an $B = 8$ bit per link width reducing the injection bandwidth to 400 MB/s (Eq. 7.1). This injection bandwidth rate was selected since it further reduced the overall network bandwidth beyond what was possible by reducing the interconnect bandwidth of the Seastar. It should also be noted that when the injection bandwidth is reduced, only the individual node is impacted. While all nodes ingress into the network are equally impacted, the network bandwidth available for routing between nodes once on the network is not reduced. A single set of baseline runs will be used and compared against identical runs while tuning the network bandwidth using the previously described methods in sequence.

---

[1] 4 rails = 1111 = 0xF, 3 rails (not used) = 0111 = 0x7, 2 rails = 0011 = 0x3, 1 rail = 0001 − 0x1.

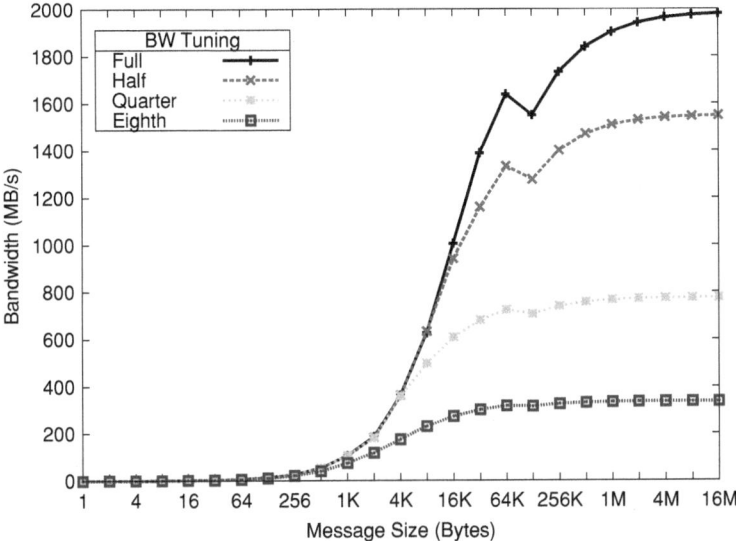

Fig. 7.1 Pallas PingPong bandwidth for all levels of network bandwidth tuning

Figure 7.1 depicts the four network bandwidth rates as measured by Pallas PingPong [2] between two dual core nodes, one core per node. As can be seen, the maximum bandwidth observed at 1/2 using these benchmarks is not 1/2 of full bandwidth. As previously mentioned, this is due to the larger interconnect bandwidth capacity as it relates to injection bandwidth. Injection bandwidth was not altered other than to achieve the 1/8th bandwidth configuration. Below 1/2 bandwidth, the steps become regular. While not perfect, when using the configuration techniques available this is the best approximation that can be achieved. It should be noted that the goal was to test at reduced network bandwidths and measure impact on performance and energy. These configurations clearly achieve this goal and represent a tunable network bandwidth capability.

The following is the sequence of experiments for the network bandwidth study:

1. Run each application at full interconnect and injection bandwidth to establish a benchmark (runtime and energy use)
2. Reboot into a 1/2 interconnect bandwidth configuration and run each application
3. Reboot into a 1/4th interconnect bandwidth configuration and run each application
4. Reboot into full interconnect bandwidth and 1/8th injection bandwidth configuration (to accomplish 1/8th network bandwidth) and run each application.

For each phase, power samples are collected (current draw and voltage) as described in Chap. 3. The scale used for each application, number of nodes and cores, is listed in Table 7.1. The results will be discussed in the following section.

No operating system modifications were necessary for either the interconnect or injection bandwidth experiments.

7.2 Results and Analysis: Network Bandwidth Tuning

The following discussion will reference Table 7.1. As in Table 6.2, increases in runtime or energy percentage are represented by positive numbers. Negative values or decreases are indicated by parenthesized numbers (all relative to the baseline values listed). Again, we were careful to use the same nodes for each application execution. Total energy includes the measured energy from the CPU, a measured energy from the Seastar, and an estimated energy from the memory subsystem. Since the memory subsystem could not be measured in isolation, the energy used by this component was calculated using a fixed wattage over time. The current draw of the entire mezzanine (the mezzanine contains four Seastar network chips, one per node) was measured but as previously stated is constant over time. This is typical of network interface controllers since the SerDes do not throttle up and down based on network traffic or on demand in current network chips. Since there are four Seastars in a single mezzanine the current reading was multiplied by the input voltage. The total was then divided by four and used as the baseline network power value for a single NIC. For 1/2, 1/4th, and 1/8th network bandwidth calculations a linear reduction in power was assumed, which had a proportional affect on total energy. For each energy value a per node use was calculated and multiplied by the number of nodes to produce the final value. The calculation is as follows (where E = Energy):

$$(E_{\text{cpu}} + E_{\text{network}} + E_{\text{memory}}) \times \text{number of nodes} = \text{Total Energy} \qquad (7.2)$$

The calculations use 25 W for the full network bandwidth value, 12.5 W for 1/2, 6.25 W for 1/4th and 3.125 W for 1/8th network bandwidth. A value of 20 W was used for the memory value based on 5 W per DIMM and four DIMMs per node. By considering all components in the calculation we avoid the network energy having a disproportional affect on the total energy calculation. While the E_{CPU} value fluctuated based on the CPU usage of the application and was measured over time, the network and memory values assumed a constant value over time. As mentioned previously, the CPU energy was measured on a large subset of the total nodes involved in the experiment. An average per node energy is calculated based on the samples from all nodes and used as the E_{CPU} value. Again note that a decrease, or savings, in energy or runtime is indicated by a parenthesized value.

Addressing each application in table order (see Table 7.1) it can be seen that the strong and weak scaling versions of SAGE have very similar characteristics. Reducing the network bandwidth by 1/2 had little affect on the runtime of both SAGE_strong (decreased by 0.593 %) and SAGE_weak (increased by 0.609 %).

Table 7.1 Experiment #2: network bandwidth: runtime and total energy % difference versus baseline

	Nodes/cores	Baseline Bandwidth (BW)		1/2 BW% Diff		1/4th BW% Diff		1/8th BW% Diff	
		Runtime (s)	Energy (J)	Runtime	Energy	Runtime	Energy	Runtime	Energy
SAGE_strong	2048/4096	337	5.79×10^7	(0.593)	(15.3)	8.90	(15.5)	20.2	(11.4)
SAGE_weak	2048/4096	328	5.64×10^7	0.609	(14.3)	8.23	(15.8)	22.6	(9.63)
CTH	2048/4096	1519	2.58×10^8	9.81	(7.09)	30.2	1.04	40.4	3.50
AMG2006	2048/4096	859	1.45×10^7	(0.815)	(15.8)	(0.116)	(22.7)	0.931	(25.9)
xNOBEL	1536/3072	533	7.01×10^7	(0.938)	(15.4)	(0.375)	(22.2)	(0.375)	(25.9)
UMT	512/1024	838	3.57×10^7	0.357	(14.7)	1.07	(21.7)	6.32	(21.8)
Charon	1024/2048	1162	9.96×10^7	1.55	(13.7)	2.15	(20.8)	2.67	(24.5)

In the same test, a significant savings in energy was observed for SAGE_strong (a decrease of 15.3%) and SAGE_weak (decrease of 14.3%). The impact on, or increase in, runtime is larger by more than 8X when the network bandwidth is reduced to 1/4th for both SAGE_strong and SAGE_weak. Little additional energy savings were observed for this test. As might be expected, further reductions to 1/8th network bandwidth for both strong and weak scaling modes of SAGE produce significant impacts on the runtime of SAGE (in excess of 20% in both modes). The accompanied energy savings using 1/8th network bandwidth is actually smaller than the 1/4th network bandwidth experiment. The difference in both runtime and energy savings between strong and weak scaling at 1/8th network bandwidth might be an indicator that additional divergence might been seen at higher scale. Based on this data, reducing network bandwidth by 1/2, if the corresponding energy consumption of the network could be reduced by half, would be advantageous for this application. Considering the runtime energy trade-off, further reductions in the network bandwidth would not be productive based on the available data.

CTH was more dramatically affected by changes in the network bandwidth than any other *real* application tested. Even at 1/2 bandwidth, CTH experiences a greater percent increase in runtime (9.81%) than is saved by reducing network energy (7.09% decrease in total energy). At 1/4th bandwidth, CTH experiences a very large increase in runtime (30.2%) accompanied by an actual increase in energy used of 1.04%. Clearly, reducing network bandwidth further is highly detrimental to both runtime and energy as can be seen from 1/8th network bandwidth results. Even at this moderately large-scale CTH requires a high performance network to execute efficiently.

AMG2006 and xNOBEL, in contrast with CTH, were insensitive to the network bandwidth changes made from the runtime perspective, which yields an opportunity for large savings in energy. Reductions down to 1/8th network bandwidth cause virtually no impact in runtime for both AMG2006 and xNOBEL while a 25.9% savings in energy can be achieved for both. (AMG2006 executed 0.931% slower while xNOBEL actually ran slightly faster, 0.375%, due to launch time variations). The savings in energy seems to be flattening by the time the network bandwidth is reduced to 1/8th. While further reductions in network bandwidth may or may not increase runtime there is likely little additional energy savings available.

UMT produced similar results to AMG2006 and xNOBEL when the network bandwidth was reduced up to 1/4th, little to no impact in runtime accompanied by a large energy savings. At 1/8th network bandwidth different characteristics were observed. UMT has a much higher impact to runtime at 1/8th network bandwidth (6.32%) than at 1/4th (1.07%) with virtually no additional energy savings (21.7% at 1/4th and 21.8% at 1/8th). The limit of network bandwidth tuning that should be applied to UMT, at least at this scale and on this platform, seems to have been located. Note, UMT was run at a smaller scale relative to the other applications. It is possible that at larger scale the results might differ.

Charon showed small, but increasing, impact on runtime as network bandwidth was reduced. At this scale it is clear that the network bandwidth could be reduced down to 1/4th with an acceptable impact in runtime (increase of 2.15%) accompanied by a very significant savings in energy (decrease of 20.8 %). Moving from 1/4th to 1/8th network bandwidth shows some signs of a flattening of energy savings but results are not conclusive. Experiments with Charon at larger scale are also warranted.

Overall, a large amount of evidence was observed to support the conjecture that a tunable NIC would be highly beneficial if corresponding energy savings resulted. In all cases but CTH, virtually no impact on runtime would be experienced by tuning the network bandwidth to 1/2. The result would be significant energy savings with little to no performance impact. In the case of AMG2006, xNOBEL and UMT the network bandwidth could be reduced to 1/4th full bandwidth with little runtime impact, allowing for even larger energy savings. These observations indicate that a tunable NIC would be beneficial but they also indicate a high performance network is critical for some applications. An ability to tune the NIC, similar to how frequency is tunable on a CPU, would be an desirable characteristic on next generation Exascale platforms.

It should be stressed that this data represents a single application running at a time. One of the reasons the interconnect bandwidth of the Seastar was designed to be greater than the injection bandwidth of a single node is that communications on networks, like the ones used on Red Storm and Jaguar, are not point to point. Often, many hops are required for a messages to travel from source to destination. Having a greater interconnect bandwidth is essential for a platform that supports a range of applications, often sharing the interconnect bandwidth. The ability to tune this component could not be exploited without considering the possible impact on other applications running on the platform, at least for network topologies like meshes and 3D-toruses. High radix network topologies with fewer hops on average could benefit more easily from a tunable network since less consideration would be necessary regarding the impact on other applications co-existing on the platform.

References

1. R. Brightwell, K. Predretti, K. Underwood, T. Hudson, SeaStar interconnect: balanced bandwidth for scalable performance. IEEE Micro **26**(3), 41–57 (2006)
2. "PALLAS", Intel, http://www.intel.com/cd/software/products/asmo-na/eng/cluster/mpi/219 848.htm

Chapter 8
Energy Delay Product

Abstract In this chapter, data from both the CPU frequency tuning experiments (Chap. 6) and the network bandwidth experiments (Chap. 7) are analyzed using a range of fused metrics based on Energy Delay Product (EDP). The analysis in this chapter demonstrates how multiple metrics can be combined and observed as a single fused metric. Additionally, a form of weighted EDP is used to more highly prioritize, or weight, performance over energy savings.

8.1 A Fused Metric

Energy Delay Product (EDP), initially proposed by Horowitz [1] to evaluate trade-offs between circuit level power saving techniques for digital designs, has been applied by Brooks [2] to more heavily, and some would argue more appropriately, weight delay by squaring or even cubing the delay factor in the calculation. Cameron, in a poster presented at SC04 [3], and in later papers, suggests a weighted approach where the delay factor can be weighted based on the priority of performance. The decision of how to weight performance versus power is largely a policy decision but in the experiments contained in this book, performance is highly valued.

The graphs in Figs. 8.1 and 8.2 were produced using the same data used to create Tables 6.2 and 7.2. In all graphs included in Figs. 8.1 and 8.2, the *Runtime* curve is produced by normalizing the runtime measured for each individual application at every P-state tested to the baseline run measured at the default P-state (P0 or P1). In Fig. 8.1 the lower x axis lists test points by P-state, the upper x axis lists test points by CPU frequency. The *Energy* curve is produced identical to the *Runtime* curve using measured CPU energy instead of measured runtime. Three EDP curves are present using the following equation:

$$E * T^w - \text{where} : E = Energy, T = Runtime \quad \text{and} \quad w = 1, 2 \text{ or } 3 \quad (8.1)$$

J. H. Laros III et al., *Energy-Efficient High Performance Computing*,
SpringerBriefs in Computer Science, DOI: 10.1007/978-1-4471-4492-2_8,
© James H. Laros III 2013

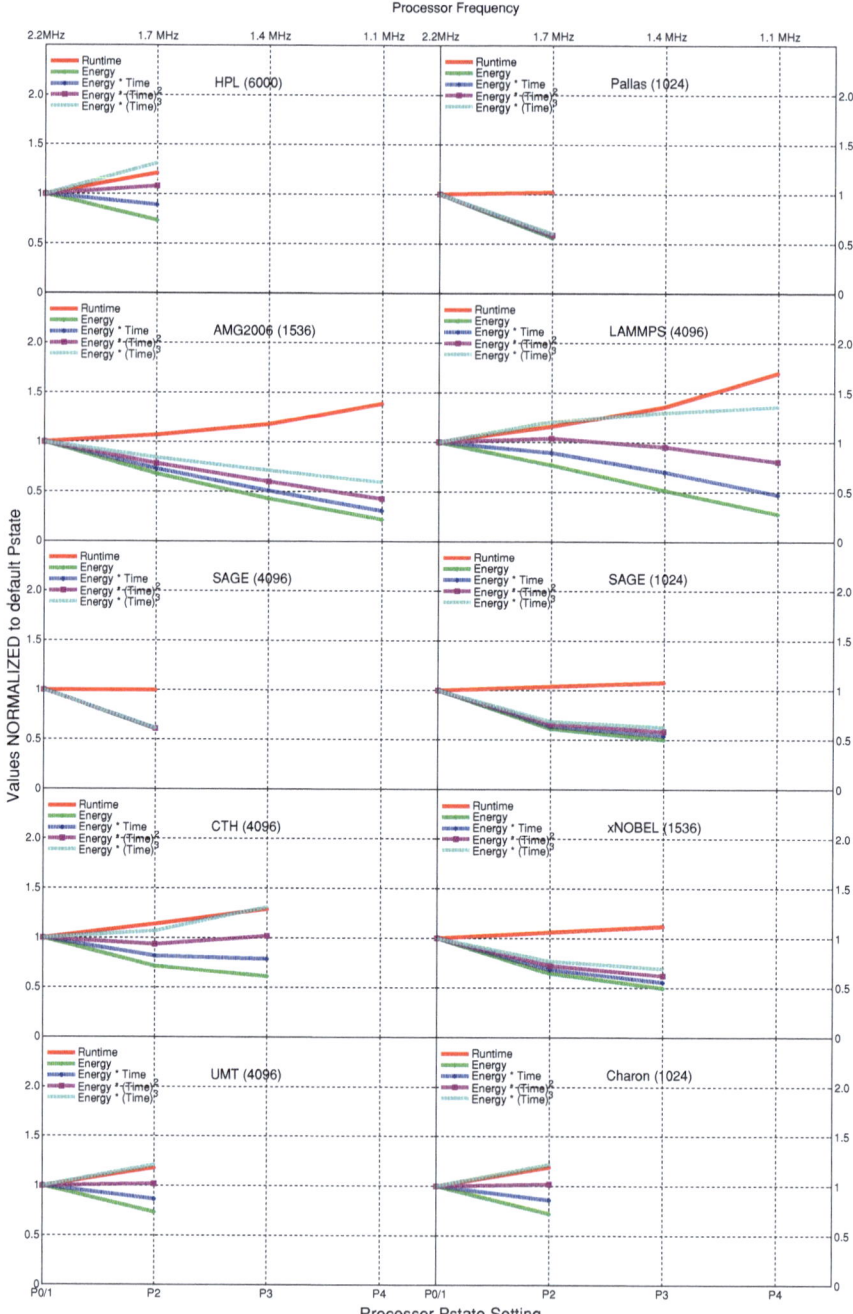

Fig. 8.1 Experiment #1: normalized energy, run-time and $E * T^w$ where $w = 1, 2,$ or 3

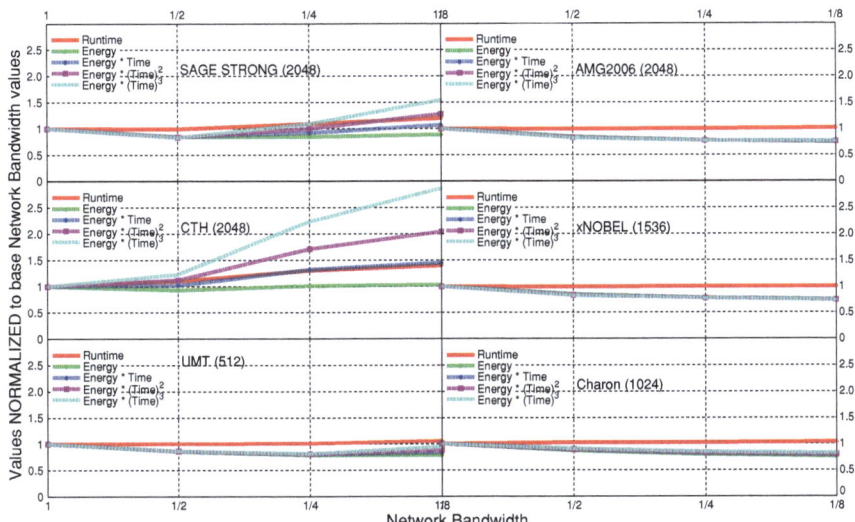

Fig. 8.2 Experiment #2: normalized total energy, run-time and $E * T^w$ where $w = 1, 2,$ or 3

All three curves are included to represent how the metric might differ depending on the weight given to time or performance. Weighting the time factor in the EDP equation seems in line with the existing priorities of HPC. As previously discussed, these priorities might change in the near future.

The HPL results show how weighting runtime (performance) moves the curve upward, indicating a less favorable trade-off as performance is more highly prioritized. Squaring the delay produces an EDP greater than one which would typically be interpreted as detrimental. It should be noted that the unweighted EDP curve trends below one. Using this metric alone HPL might productively be run at a lower P-state. This should be an indication that if performance is a priority the unweighted EDP metric might not be appropriate. The Pallas graph, however, shows that even if the delay is cubed this metric indicates a benefit running at P-state 2.

While the results for HPL and Pallas are mostly in line with previous observations, some of the real application results could be interpreted differently. Even based on the EDP cubed metric, AMG2006, for example, appears to benefit when executed at any P-state including P-state 4. This differs from the analysis in Chap. 6 based on separate runtime and energy differences listed in Table 6.2. The previous conclusion was that a 39.1 % hit in runtime would not be acceptable. Considering the percentage hit in runtime in isolation 39.1 % does sound extreme, but considering the actual runtime value the EDP metric exposes a dimension that might otherwise have been ignored. The runtime for AMG2006 is very short in these experiments. Recall, it was noted that the fastest runs in P-state 2 actually took less time than the slowest runs measured in P-state 1. Since the runtime for AMG2006 is so short, a 39.1 % hit in runtime only increases the runtime by approximately 68 seconds. When dealing with very short runtimes even cubing the delay in the EDP equation might not be enough.

If the cubed EDP is used as a metric for the remaining applications the resulting analysis closely resembles the initial analysis based on the separate energy and runtime differences (Table 6.2). In conclusion, lowering the CPU frequency for CTH, UMT, and Charon is detrimental, while SAGE and xNOBEL are less sensitive to CPU frequency changes.

The graphs in Fig. 8.2 represent the runtime and total energy measurements produced from the data used in Chap. 7. The *Runtime* and *Energy* curves are normalized in the same manner as described for Fig. 8.1 with the exception that total energy is measured as described in Eq. 7.2. EDP is calculated using Eq. 8.1 using total energy. The x axis lists the steps of network bandwidth reduction. The EDP curves, again, generally represent the previous analysis. SAGE is not sensitive to the initial network bandwidth reduction to 1/2 but quickly trends negative as bandwidth is reduced further. CTH is very sensitive to all network bandwidth changes. AMG2006, xNOBEL, UMT, and Charon in contrast are generally insensitive to network bandwidth changes. Recall, however, additional judgments were previously stated based on the analysis of the separate energy and runtime metrics listed in Table 8.2. In the case of UMT, diminishing returns were noted as network bandwidth was decreased. The curves trend upward as 1/8th network bandwidth is approached. This seemed easier to identify when analyzing the tabularized data. Regardless, this method of analyzing data can help to develop a quick impression of the trends. If further analysis is warranted the raw data can be consulted.

For HPC, the EDP cubed equation is most appropriate due to the focus on performance. Possibly the performance factor of the metric should be weighted even higher to better represent the performance priority of HPC workloads. Bounding an equation such as EDP could be productive. For example, if a upper limit on the wall-clock time for an application is desired, the EDP equation might indicate what level of tuning can be applied while meeting the runtime requirements. Likewise, if the amount of energy used during a certain period is limited, it would be possible to calculate the expected turnaround time for a particular application.

Many different considerations may be taken into account as data centers migrate to more energy efficient operation. Time of day, for example, might be an important consideration. Power is often much more expensive during daylight or business hours. Scheduling decisions, or which applications run when, might be based on how efficient they can be executed. For example, applications could be evaluated and assigned an energy efficiency value. During high power cost hours, it may be determined that only applications that are 90 % efficient or better may be executed. Another possibility is the amount of power that can be delivered to a data center, either generally or again at certain times of day. Hypothetically, applications might be executed at reduced frequencies just to keep the maximum power draw of the platform below predetermined limits. These and other considerations could become common practice in HPC data centers. While the policies enforced at data centers may differ widely, the underlying mechanisms of measurement, and the ability to affect power use are common.

References

1. M. Horowitz, T. Indermaur, R. Gonzalez, Low-power digital design, in *Proceedings of the IEEE Symposium on Low Power Electronics*, 1994
2. D. Brooks, P. Bose, S. Schuster, H. Jacobson, P. Kudva, A. Buyuktosunoglu, J. Wellman, V. Zyuban, M. Gupta, P. Cook, Power-aware microarchitecture: design and modeling challenges for next-generation microprocessors. IEEE Micro **20**(6), 26–44 (2000)
3. K.W. Cameron, R. Ge, X. Feng, D. Varner, C. Jones, POSTER: high-performance, power-aware distributed computing framework, in *Proceedings of the International Conference on High Performance Computing, Networking, Storage, and Analysis (SC)*, ACM/IEEE, 2004

Chapter 9
Conclusions

> *...not everything that can be counted counts, and not everything that counts can be counted.*
>
> William Bruce Cameron

One of the primary conclusions drawn from our research is the importance of the ability to measure power at large scale without affecting the experiment being conducted. Previously, empirical power and energy analysis at the scale of these experiments has not been possible. This research began by targeting low hanging fruit in the form of power savings during idle cycles. The measuring capability was fine-tuned and the effects that the operating system modifications had were easily observed including quantifying the impact of noise on power. Additionally, a capability to characterize application energy use was developed. This initial work yielded significant rewards and prompted further research as described in this book.

While it was initially assumed that a dynamic approach to tuning platform components would be necessary to achieve a beneficial trade-off between performance and energy, it was discovered that large initial gains could result from a simpler static approach. Static tuning has many advantages including stability. Dynamic tuning, at scale, has the potential to be difficult to manage. If not done properly dynamic tuning could introduce reliability issues or diminishing benefits for performance and/or energy. Dynamic frequency scaling, of any component, also requires consideration of how long it takes to accomplish the desired frequency changes. If transitions are too frequent the resulting overhead could negate any potential gain. It is likely that many applications will require dynamic tuning to achieve energy savings while maintaining acceptable levels of performance. Whether static or dynamic, the results of these experiments indicate that a system level approach is essential for achieving positive results for scientific computing applications run at large scale.

The experiments conducted have shown applications like AMG2006 and xNO-BEL to be largely insensitive to CPU frequency reductions. Both AMG2006 and xNOBEL also proved to be tolerant of network bandwidth reductions. It is possible that if both the CPU frequency and network bandwidth were tuned at the same time

J. H. Laros III et al., *Energy-Efficient High Performance Computing*, SpringerBriefs in Computer Science, DOI: 10.1007/978-1-4471-4492-2_9, © James H. Laros III 2013

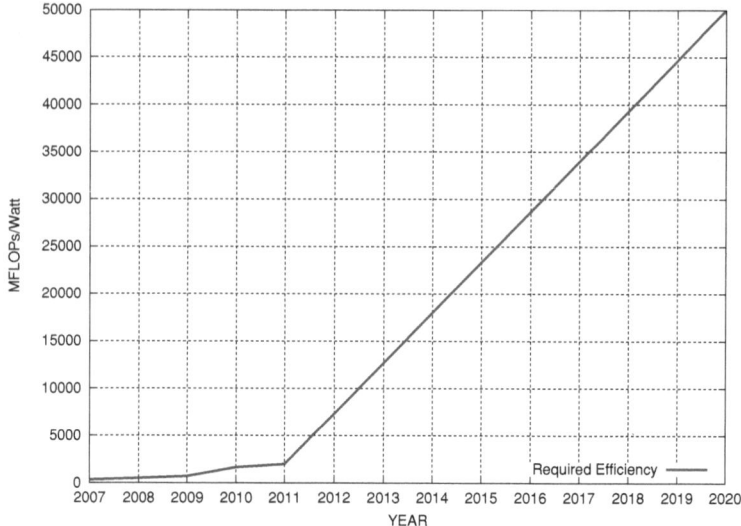

Fig. 9.1 Required power efficiency to reach 1 ExaFLOP using under 20 MW of power

even greater energy savings could be realized. Using xNOBEL as an example, if the per node energy value from the CPU frequency analysis at P-state 2 is applied to the total energy calculation for the 1/8th network bandwidth experiment, xNOBEL would experience a total of 56.4 % increase in energy savings with a 6 % impact in runtime. Numbers could be projected for every application but experimental results are the most meaningful.

xNOBEL was specifically selected in the previous example since it was the least impacted by any tuning applied. CTH, however, was significantly affected by CPU frequency adjustments. If CPU frequency was reduced while executing CTH could the network bandwidth be reduced without further impact on runtime? Would this result in additional energy savings making the runtime impact more palatable? Possibly, if memory or some other component is the bottleneck, but this cannot be definitively stated.

This research indicates each application has a *sweet spot* based on its computation and communication requirements. Additionally, it has been observed that energy savings and runtime are impacted, sometimes significantly, by scale. The trade-offs are platform and application specific—when one bottleneck is removed, another will appear, and the order the bottlenecks appear will depend on the platform. Conducting these experiments on an architecture like the Cray XT/XE/XK is valuable since it is well-balanced in its default configuration [1]. As a result of these experiments, we can conclude that components on future HPC platforms should be as tunable as possible and under software control so that end-users or system software can optimize the energy/performance tradeoff on a per application basis. A systems level approach is essential for success on HPC platforms.

   Unprecedented improvements in energy efficiency must occur in the next decade
to accomodate practical limitations of powering next generation platforms.
Figure 9.1 plots the most energy efficient platforms from 2007 through 2011 in terms
of MFLOPs/Watt. If the practical or imposed [2] limitation of a platform targeted to
reach one ExaFLOP in the year 2020 is 20 MW the required energy efficiency would
be 50,000 MFLOPs/Watt. This represents an approximately 25X increase in energy
efficiency in the 9 years between 2011 and 2020. In contrast, the last 4 years have
produced only a 6X improvement. Hardware must provide the bulk of the needed
improvement in energy efficiency, but how the hardware is used and controlled by
software will be critically important to reaching long-term energy efficiency goals.

References

1. R. Brightwell, K. Predretti, K. Underwood, T. Hudson, SeaStar interconnect: balanced bandwidth
   for scalable performance. IEEE Micro. **26**(3), 41–57 (2006)
2. K. Bergman, S. Borkar, D. Campbell, W. Carlson, W. Dally, M. Denneau, P. Franzon, W. Harrod,
   J. Hiller, S. Karp, S. Keckler, D. Klein, R. Lucas, M. Richards, A. Scarpelli, S. Scott, A. Snavely,
   T. Sterling, R. S. Williams, K. Yelick, Exascale computing study: technology challenges in
   achieving exascale systems peter kogge, editor and study lead, 2008

References

1. R. Brightwell, B.W. Barrett, K.S. Hemmert, K.D. Underwood. Challenges for high-performance networking for exascale computing, in *Proceedings of the International Conference on Computer Communications and Networks (ICCCN)*. IEEE, 2010
2. D.M. Brooks, P. Bose, S.E. Schuster, H. Jacobson, P.N. Kudva, A. Buyuktosunoglu, J. Wellman, V. Zyuban, M. Gupta, P.W. Cook, Power-aware microarchitecture: design and modeling challenges for next-generation microprocessors. IEEE Micro **20**(6), 26–44 (2000)
3. F. Bellosa, The benefits of event-driven energy accounting in power-sensitive systems, in *SIGOPS, European Workshop*. ACM, 2000
4. W.L. Bircher, L.K. John, Complete system power estimation: a trickle-down approach based on performance events, in *Proceedings of the International Symposium on Performance Analysis of Systems & Software, (ISPASS)*. IEEE, 2007
5. R. Brightwell, K.T. Predretti, K.D. Underwood, T. Hudson, Seastar interconnect: balanced bandwidth for scalable performance. IEEE Micro **26**(3), 41–57 (2006)
6. R. Brightwell, K.D. Underwood, C. Vaughan, J. Stevenson, Performance evaluation of the Red Storm dual-core upgrade. Concurr. Comput. Pract. Exper. **22**(2), 175–190 (2010)
7. W.L. Bircher, M. Valluri, J. Law, L. John, Runtime identification of microprocessor energy saving opportunities, in *Proceedings of the International Symposium on Low Power Electronics and Design, (ISLPED)*. ACM, 2005
8. K.W. Cameron, R. Ge, X. Feng, D. Varner, C. Jones, POSTER: High-performance, power-aware distributed computing framework, in *Proceedings of the International Conference on High Performance Computing, Networking, Storage, and Analysis (SC)*. ACM/IEEE, 2004
9. J. Dongarra, J. Bunch, C. Moler, G. W. Stewart, High performance linpack HPL. In Technical Report CS-89-85. University of Tennessee, 1989
10. K.B. Ferreira, R. Brightwell, P.G. Bridges, Characterizing application sensitivity to OS interference using Kernel-level noise Injection, in *Proceedings of the International Conference on High Performance Computing, Networking, Storage, and Analysis (SC)*. ACM/IEEE, 2008
11. X. Feng, R. Ge, K.W. Cameron, Power and energy profiling on scientific applications on distributed systems, in *Proceedings of the International Parallel and Distributed Processing Symposium (IPDPS)*. IEEE, 2005
12. R.D. Falgout, P.S. Vassilevski, On generalizing the AMG framework. Soc. Ind. Appl. Math. SIAM J. Numer. Anal. **42**(4), 1669–1693 (2003)
13. R. Ge, X. Feng, K.W. Cameron, Improvement of power-performance efficiency for high-end computing, in *Proceedings of the International Parallel and Distributed Processing Symposium (IPDPS)*. IEEE, 2005

14. R. Ge, X. Feng, K.W. Cameron, Performance-constrained distributed DVS scheduling for scientific applications on power-aware clusters. In *Proceedings of the International Conference on High Performance Computing, Networking, Storage, and Analysis (SC)*. ACM/IEEE, 2005

15. R. Ge, X. Feng, S. Song, H.-C. Chang, D. Li, K.W. Cameron, PowerPack: energy profiling and analysis of high-performance systems and applications. Trans. Parallel Distrib. Syst. **21**(5), 658–671 (2010)

16. M. Gittings, R. Weaver, M. Clover, T. Betlach, N. Byrne, R. Coker, E. Dendy, R. Hueckstaedt, K. New, W.R. Oakes, D. Ranta, R. Stefan, The RAGE radiation-hydrodynamic code. J. Comput. Sci. Discov. **1**(1), 015005 (2008)

17. C. Hsu, W. Feng, Power-aware run-time system for high-performance computing, in *Proceedings of the International Conference on High Performance Computing, Networking, Storage, and Analysis (SC)*. ACM/IEEE, 2005

18. M. Horowitz, T. Indermaur, R. Gonzalez, Low-power digital design, in *Proceedings of the Symposium on Low Power Electronics*. IEEE, 1994

19. E.S. Hertel Jr, R.L. Bell, M.G. Elrick, A.V. Farnsworth, G.I. Kerley, J.M. Mcglaun, S.V. Petney, S.A. Silling, P.A. Taylor, L. Yarrington, CTH: a software family for multi-dimensional shock physics analysis, in *Proceedings of the International Symposium on Shock Waves*. NTIS, 1993

20. C. Hsu, U. Kremer, The design, implementation, and evaluation of a compiler algorithm for CPU energy reduction, in *Proceedings of the Conference on Programming Language Design and Implementation, (PLDI)*. ACM, 2003

21. S.M. Kelly, R.B. Brightwell, Software Architecture of the Light Weight Kernel, Catamount, in *Cray User Group*. CUG, 2005

22. Kitten Light Weight Kernel, Sandia National Laboratories. Available https://software.sandia.gov/trac/kitten

23. A. Kodi, A. Louri, Performance adaptive power-aware reconfigurable optical interconnects for high-performance computing (HPC) systems, in *Proceedings of the International Conference on High Performance Computing, Networking, Storage, and Analysis (SC)*. ACM/IEEE, 2007

24. S. Kamil, J. Shalf, E. Strohmaier, Power efficiency in high performance computing, in *Proceedings of the International Parallel and Distributed Processing Symposium (IPDPS)*. IEEE, 2008

25. D. Li, B.R. de Supinski, M. Schulz, K. Cameron, D.S. Nikolopoulos, Hybrid MPI/OpenMP power-aware computing, in *Proceedings of the International Parallel and Distributed Processing Symposium (IPDPS)*. IEEE, 2010

26. J.H. Laros III, A software and hardware architecture for a modular, portable, extensible reliability availability and serviceability system, in *Proceedings of the Workshop on High Performance Computing Reliability Issues*. IEEE, 2006

27. D. Li, D.S. Nikolopoulos, K. Cameron, B.R. de Supinski, M. Schulz, Power-aware MPI task aggregation prediction for high-end computing systems, in *Proceedings of the International Parallel and Distributed Processing Symposium (IPDPS)*. IEEE, 2010

28. P.T. Lin, J.N. Shadid, M. Sala, R.S. Tuminaro, G.L. Hennigan, R.J. Hoekstra, Performance of a parallel algebraic multilevel preconditioner for stabilized finite element semiconductor device modeling. J. Comput. Phys. **228**, 6250–6267 (2009)

29. S.A. McKee, Reflections on the memory wall. In *Proceedings of the Conference on Computing Frontiers, CF '04*. ACM, 2004

30. K. Pedretti, R. Brightwell, D. Doerfler, K. Hemmert, J. Laros, The impact of injection bandwidth performance on application scalability, in *Proceedings of the European MPI Users' Group Conference on Recent Advances in the Message Passing Interface*. Springer, 2011

31. F. Petrini, D. Kerbyson, S. Pakin, The Case of the missing supercomputer performance: achieving optimal performance on the 8,192 processors of ASCI Q, in *Proceedings of the International Conference on High Performance Computing, Networking, Storage, and Analysis (SC)*. ACM/IEEE, 2003

32. S. Plimpton, Fast parallel algorithms for short-range molecular dynamics. J. Comput. Phys. **117**, 1–19 (1995)

33. E. Pinheiro, W.-D. Weber, L.A. Barroso. Failure trends in a large disk drive population, in *Proceedings of the 5th USENIX conference on File and Storage Technologies*. USENIX, 2007

34. L. Shang, L.-S. Peh, N.K. Jha, Dynamic voltage scaling with links for power optimization of interconnection networks, in *Proceedings of the International Symposium on High-Performance Computer Architecture, (HPCA)*. IEEE, 2003

35. C.T. Vaughan, J.P. VanDyke, S.M. Kelly, Application performance under different XT operating systems, in *Cray User Group*. CUG, 2008

36. D.W. Wall, Limits of instruction-level parallelism, in *SIGARCH Computer Architecture News*, vol. 19. ACM, 1991

37. R. Weaver, M. Gittings, Massively Parallel Simulations with DOE's ASCI Supercomputers: An Overview of the Los Alamos Crestone Project. In *Adaptive Mesh Refinement—Theory and Applications*, Springer, Berlin, Heidelberg, 2005

38. M. White, *Microelectronics Reliability: Physics-of-Failure Based Modeling and Lifetime Evaluation*. Jet Propulsion Laboratory, National Aeronautics and Space Administration, 2008

39. A. Zavanella, A. Milazzo, Predictability of bulk synchronous programs using MPI, in *Proceedings of the Euromicro Workshop on Parallel and Distributed Processing*. IEEE, 2000

40. R. Zajcew, P. Roy, D. Black, C. Peak, P. Guedes, B. Kemp, J. LoVerso, M. Leibensperger, M. Barnett, F. Rabii, D. Netterwala, An OSF/1 UNIX for massively parallel multicomputers, in *Proceedings of the USENIX Technical Conference*. USENIX, 1993

Index

J. H. Laros III et al., *Energy-Efficient High Performance Computing*,
SpringerBriefs in Computer Science, DOI: 10.1007/978-1-4471-4492-2,
© James H. Laros III 2013